T0156849

PENNIES ON THE ROAD

BY ROBERT W. PERRAS

A novel based upon a true story.

iUniverse, Inc.
New York   Bloomington

Pennies on the Road

iUniverse books may be ordered through booksellers or by contacting:

iUniverse
1663 Liberty Drive
Bloomington, IN 47403
www.iuniverse.com
1-800-Authors (1-800-288-4677)

Because of the dynamic nature of the Internet, any Web addresses or links contained in this book may have changed since publication and may no longer be valid. The views expressed in this work are solely those of the author and do not necessarily reflect the views of the publisher, and the publisher hereby disclaims any responsibility for them.

ISBN: 978-1-4502-6578-2 (sc)
ISBN: 978-1-4502-6581-2 (ebook)
ISBN: 978-1-4502-6582-9 (hc)

Printed in the United States of America

iUniverse rev. date: 10/18/2010

Contents

Chapter One
Day One

The morgue was appropriately cold and ineffably dreary, much as you would expect any morgue to be. I hadn't been there too long. I knew very little of morgues. Truth is, I knew nothing about morgues, and even less about where I was. All I knew at this point was that I was cold, I was alone and I'd better start raising a ruckus if I was to change my situation.

They told me some years later, that soon after I was born, they were not able to discern any heartbeat so; evidently, I made that short trip from delivery room, to the morgue downstairs. When told the heartbreaking news about her newborn baby boy, my mother, in total hysterics, demanded that she see and hold her baby one last time.

Moments later, in an effort to pacify this frantic patient, they discovered in a tiny basket, a very angry baby furiously kicking off his tiny shroud. I had been born with arrhythmia, also an abnormally slow heartbeat (twenty-six at rest) and in later years developed sleep apnea. Combined, all three helped carve a few distinct bends in my road, starting with day one.

Author Bobbie   *Age 8 months*

Needless to say, I actually remember nothing of the above incident. This was only one of the myriad stories told to me over a half century or so. To start this story at the beginning, which seems like a good place to start, I will have to rely on many and varying tales told to me by those who allegedly were there. The validity of their recounts I have no reason not to accept as truth.

However, the incidents related in first person, I can attest to, allowing perhaps some degree of memory enhancement. This then, is my story, as I remember it.

Jean Gwendolyn Phyllis Wright

1937 Mother Gwen

My mother Jean Gwendolyn Wright, in her teenage years, was a fine figure of a woman. Her sisters said she was a Rhonda Fleming redhead with a figure to match. Another time, another place, she might have made a name for herself in Hollywood.

Her mother, Anna and father, William, had their hands full with her two brothers and three sisters. Unlike her sisters, Margaret, Pat and Marion, Gwen decided early in life to free herself from family responsibilities and move on to bigger and better things. The depression was over and jobs were becoming more available. Gasoline was only twenty cents a gallon, stamps two cents and Walt Disney released his first full length feature, Snow White. So much happening, so much to do. Schooling held little appeal, but making money did. Unfortunately, as most of us learned much too late in life, limited schooling severely limits one's future employment opportunities.

A series of nondescript jobs eventually had her looking elsewhere for personal worth and satisfaction. The hotels, with their separate pubs for men and women became her chosen domain. As soon as her work was through, she would rush home, change to a figure accenting outfit, highlight her hazel eyes and vigorously brush her long, auburn hair and then hurry to her favorite playground, the Leonard Hotel in beautiful downtown St. Catharines.

Big entrances probably gave her a lot of self satisfaction. Entering the Hotel and sashaying across the lobby towards the "Women & Escorts" entrance, she just knew every male eye was watching her closely. She also knew that, several of the women were watching her. It's possible though, that they were not watching with the envy that she happily assumed. But, she really didn't care what they thought anyway. She was trolling for the male eyes.

Albert's Boys

The Perras Barbershop

My grandfather, Albert Perras had five sons. He was a respectable and much admired barber in Ottawa and later in St. Catharines, Ontario. Clients had been getting their trims from him since the end of the last century.

Ottawa, on the waterfront would never have been most people's choice for the perfect environment to raise a family. The neighborhood was predominantly French with strong Catholic morals. Albert, purportedly a holdover from the old school, ruled his boys with an iron hand, presumably, as required.

The Perras Boys

However, when the back of the hand wasn't deemed adequate punishment for the crime, the leather strap he used for stropping his straight razors served the purpose. Five inches wide and two feet long, it became a formidable enforcer, in the hands of a skilled user.

For Albert Junior, John, Leon, Marcel and young Ralph, it was usually enough of a deterrent, to assure that only the most foolish would become a repeat offender. As Albert struggled to control his son's bodies, the Catholic Church strived to control and save their souls.

The mandatory penance dispensed by the Priests and the obligatory time in the confessionals of the Catholic church, after a night or two of reveling, did little to curtail their quest for ways out of Ottawa.

Anywhere, away from home and the French community. In fact it may have added impetus to the quest for a new and anarchical lifestyle. Eventually, all five brothers gave up on their schooling and headed for the steel mills in Ontario.

Unfortunately, there was not a lot of opportunity for young men who didn't speak English. So the first priority was to learn English, second, get a job, and third, hopefully, find a good woman.

Father Ralph   1937

My father Ralph was the baby in the family. Four older brothers to pick on him and order him around. Four older brothers who wore the clothes first. Shoes that had been worn by everyone, first. Underwear that would never see white again. But when you're the baby, you don't spend too much time analyzing, yet you do wonder occasionally, if someday you just might get to wear something brand new. By the time he reached the teenage years, he had a new more important problem to deal with. He had stopped growing at only five-six. Added to this unfortunate burden was that he was overweight. However, in spite of the height and weight dilemmas, Ralph was a handsome man with a lot of ladies' appeal. He lived for the good times. Unfortunately he was an emotional disaster waiting to happen.

The steel mills in St Catharines offered good pay, long hours and many opportunities to meet new people who already spoke English. Ralph, although the smallest was surprisingly, most outgoing. He quickly learned the language and he just as quickly learned the ropes. After his first day on the job, he was invited by his new pals to join them for a few pints at the local pub at the Leonard Hotel on St. Paul Street. Ralph was most happy to accept the invitation. The first payday was still several days away. But, he'd worry about that later. The job would always be there, but drinking buddies in the pub, well, everyone knows that friends are more important than work. And so, with a draft in one hand and a cigarette in the other, and an eye for the women, Ralph Perras had, early in life, presumably found his career.

The Wright Sisters

Gwen left the restaurant early and nearly missed the cross-town trolley. St. Catharines, in the thirties, was not a large city, but it was much too spread out to walk across. The few pennies that it cost to ride the length of Central to downtown, were well worth it. Besides, it gave her the opportunity to look at all the displays in the windows of the shops. Shops she hoped someday to actually go inside. The mannequins seemed to call out to her, with outstretched arms and their Paris style hairdos. Fancy dresses slid magically across her body as the passing displays filled her head with visions of her grand entrances. So alluring was her daydream that she almost missed her stop at the Dominion Building on Queen Street. Jumping up she pulled the cord and ran to the trolley steps. At the corner, waiting was her sister Marion. Marion laughed out loud as she watched Gwen scramble to get to the exit in time. Fantasy and daydreams would have to wait. She had promised Marion a high time on the town tonight and she jumped from the trolley, practically falling into her sister's arms!

Marion was the oldest of the four sisters. She was the plain vanilla one. Marion would marry for love. Younger sister Margaret was considered the brains. Pat, the quiet one, never made waves and most times blended into the background. She was voted most likely to marry, raise 2.4 kids and live happily ever after. Gwen ever the opportunist would vie for romance and excitement. Mother Mae Wright's working schedule left little time for inter-family socializing. She worked two jobs from early morning through the evening hours. Thus the girls were left to generate their own pleasures and futures.

By the time Marion reached her twenties she had made a wise choice. Her first and only love, Mark provided her with security and family, but, unfortunately, later in life she became plagued with health problems. Mark found himself relegated to become a lifetime caretaker-husband.

Margaret met and married Johnnie, a bigger than life dreamer, on whose dreams they kept pinning their future plans. His early death left Margaret with a large void of emptiness and loneliness. In later life she began to fill the too many solitary hours with booze and cigarettes. Margaret's early marriage caused Gwen a certain degree of jealousy. She decided it was time to concentrate her attentions to the most current pool of available male genes, The Leonard Hotel in downtown St. Catharines.

The Land of Leonard

Hotels, in Canada, in the thirties were more than simply abodes for weary travelers. Most had some sort of neon beacon, beckoning both the timid and the curious, to come in and check us out. Rooms for rent and beer and booze! But in the thirties, all was well within the proscribed parameters of the decorum of the day. The pubs were well defined by the signs, "Men Only" and "Ladies and Escorts". The "Ladies" side permitted men, but only if they were escorted by a lady. The presumption was that all females on that side were ladies. Some cared more about getting a date for Saturday night, than being viewed as ladies. The obvious drawback was that men could not walk around the women's side and of course, the women couldn't troll the men's side. The obvious answer was to find an available female friend to sit at the table nearest the door. That way any available male standing in the doorway might have a chance of being invited in. A methodology Gwen was already too familiar with.

Marion frequently chided Gwen for her openly flirting with each guy as he peered through the open door. She need not have worried though. Most of the young men stealing furtive glances through the doorway were probably more nervous than any possible threat to the women. One by one they came, they looked and they retreated. Another night was wasted talking with her sister. Gwen began to think there has to be a better way to meet that man of her dreams.

Chapter Two
My Name is Ralph

The Facilitator of your Dreams

Across the Lobby, in the Men's side, Ralph was sitting at a table with two of his buddies, telling bawdy jokes and generally trying to impress them with his knowledge of the art of the pick-up. Casual conversations eventually grew more serious as the evening hours wore on and the window of opportunity slowly closed. All had at least two or three times, prowled the doorway to the women's side. All had returned with the same answers. Nothing worth going after. Earlier, there were thirty to forty females in the women's side and by now that excuse was wearing thin. It was time for the man of the group to stand up and show the others who was the master at pick-up. One last glass of beer, on top of the other uncounted glasses and Ralph was ready.

Gwen & Ralph

Through the open door, Ralph could see that the room has thinned out. Maybe only twelve to fifteen left. He leaned against the doorway, scanning above the heads, hoping no one would catch his eye. Slowly his gaze circled the room, back to the door. Beside him was the redhead. She was a knockout. No sense even hitting on her. She'd drop him after his first line. He looked behind. The guys were watching. Faced with failure in front of the guys or ego busting from the redhead? What a decision. Ralph, on leaded legs, moved in. He mentally phrased his opening line, "Hi Red, my name is Ralph, and I'm from Ottawa".

Gwen watched the embers on her Players' cigarette burn to a white ash. Marion was in another world, staring deep into her glass. She had just dropped a bombshell on her sister. She said she'd decided that she was going to join the Army. Gwen contemplated the news for a moment. This scene was boring, maybe Marion was right. Maybe she should sign up too. The usual din of laughing females slowly dropped to an almost inaudible level. She was alone with her thoughts. Work was a drag, her sisters and friends were all getting married, why not her? This was the wrong dress for this place. How soon can I get out of here? The ash fell. She watched it dissolve into the spilled ale. From somewhere above the fog of self contemplation, a man's voice brought her back. She looked up and smiled as the daring young man, fidgeted nervously awaiting her response. Though a most inauspicious beginning, it was indeed most opportune. Gwen and Ralph's meeting that night was the beginning. From that moment in time, I began my life's journey.

The Family

It's not known, the number of days, nights, weeks or even months until Gwen and Ralph made their union official. Some say a year other say less. But all agree it was long, drawn out and most tempestuous. Ralph proudly brought Gwen home to meet his family. In reality, mostly to show off his trophy date. The brothers were of mixed opinions. Albert Junior and John smiled politely. Leon scoffed at Gwen's obvious lack of social amenities. But Marcel, the other short brother, found her fascinating.

Ralph meanwhile, still scanning the availables, in the dating pool, had found another apparently more interesting young lady, named Lucille, and summarily abandoned Gwen. For several months it was Marcel and Gwen until Marcel met Lucille. She stole his heart and Gwen was, once again history. Fortunately, for me, Ralph was once again available and so the two began anew.

June 20th. 1936

In June 1936 they married. During the next four years, she recorded at least four pregnancies. Three ending in miscarriages.

Accidental falls down stairs, tripping off curbs, and falling in general were reasons for her pregnancy failures. But, nature had her way, and eventually Gwen carried the only child that actually made it past the portal to humankind.

And one fine day in June, a baby boy, Robert William Albert Perras was delivered. My troubles started early. I barely made it out of the morgue.

Chapter Three
The Very Early Years

A Slight Bend in the Road

Harry & Bobby

The first distinct turn of events, most of which I barely remember, was when I was just a baby. I would be taken to a park, just down the street from where we lived. A large man, with a big belly, at least from my perspective, would take my baby fingers in his giant hand and patiently walk me along the streets of St. Catharines till we reached a special grassy oasis. There, we would sit together upon an aging green park bench. He would tell me about the squirrels, the robins and the puppies, playing across the knolls. I would crawl all over him, like scaling my very own mountain. He gave me a sense of security. Though I didn't know it at the time, it was the most secure I would ever feel for many years to come. I loved my big Uncle Harry.

Sadly it wasn't till some fifty years later, that I learned that he not only wasn't my Uncle Harry, but, he was no relation whatsoever. So much for fond childhood memories.

Gwen and Ralph led an interesting life. Neither liked the idea of working eight hours a day, six days a week. Both felt there should be more to life than just working. Their efforts to find that elusive extra, led only to more discontent. Their jobs in the workplace suffered and their harmony in the home deteriorated. Ralph gained weight. Perhaps from his propensity for beer. Gwen's love of silks and fine clothes led to even more discontent regarding Ralph's income limitations. Their inevitable end was most foreseeable. The additional encumbrance of an unwanted child was burdening. The infinite joys of the omnipresent party, was far more magnetizing than the ever present responsibilities of parenthood.

The Women & Escorts romance was rapidly deteriorating into an irreparable situation. Ralph and Gwen probably loved each other. They assumed that their love would endure forever. Most new lovers feel that way. Sadly, the everlasting vows of Ralph and Gwen eventually succumbed to a new pressure. The evil of "I deserve better" began its decay. It became impossible to please each other. Each faulting the other. Perhaps he might find what he wanted in the bottom of a bottle, but could she ever find what she was looking for? Did she even know? Ralph's drinking never provided him the relief he sought from his own inadequacies.

Eventually, like so many other young men, at the time, he decided to join the army and see the world. His decision and subsequent absence opened new doors for Gwen at her favorite haunt, the Leonard Hotel.

Ralph Loses

Ralph, after returning from overseas, drifted from one menial job to another. Their marriage ended and his ill chosen path, totally without direction, ultimately led to his untimely demise.

He never remarried and led a solitary, booze enhanced life style. He had almost reached the age of fifty when he died on the operating table, from a blot clot, during an operation on his leg. He, incidentally, had been an alcoholic for over two decades, when he passed away at the St. Catharines General Hospital.

As an aside it's interesting to note that in attendance at Ralph's funeral were his four older brothers, Albert Junior, Leon, Marcel, and John, their respective spouses and his parents and an assortment of nieces and nephews. Most all the Perras clan was there. Except me! No one had bothered to inform me of his passing. I learned of his demise from his landlady.

She returned to me, a letter I had mailed him a week before his operation. After his death, she opened and read it. She was shocked to learn that no one bothered to notify me of his death or the funeral. She was aware that I had been in constant touch with Ralph, over the years. Since I was a teenager, I had visited and written to him, countless times, when he lived over the bar, in Port Colborne. She expressed her shock when she wrote to me in Florida advising me of what no one in the family felt obligated to do. Needless to say, I was terribly angry and hurt.

The Englishman

Gwen's new status, free and almost divorced allowed her to enjoy the company of many potential suitors.

A young English immigrant, James Burnett was ready and waiting in the wings. Perhaps, he just might provide the sought after relief for her yearnings for the glamorous life. She hadn't yet achieved any of the fame and recognition that she craved, but, maybe this time she would strike pay dirt.

England in 1907 was not the picturesque local that today's movies portray. At the turn of the century, it was dirty, constantly damp, gray and depressing. Thick eye-burning smoke from the thousands of chimneys blotted out the few times the sun almost shone. Ten months of the year, the wet cold wrapped you in an unforgiving blanket. To a boy, born just a stone's throw from the docks, the allure of escaping the rampant pauperism and getting on one of those ships leaving port daily, was constantly beckoning.

Jim Burnett, The Englishman

Little James Burnett, son of a bootblack, and now orphaned was only fourteen years old. He was barely five feet tall, not yet a hundred pounds. After weeks of prowling the waterfronts, he discovered the opportunity of his lifetime. The Canadian government was offering free passage to Canada in return for being a government paid farm hand. Fresh air, warm sunshine and great working conditions. What could be better? Canada would allow him to shake off England's mud, cold and dreariness and open new opportunities for him.

Twenty-six days later, after pulling a man's shift in the bowels of the ship and enduring constant sea-sickness, a tired and aching James, Burnett landed in Montreal. As his foot touched Canadian soil, his ear-to-ear grin of relief changed instantly to wide-eyed shock. Everyone, except him, spoke French!

The Roller Coaster Begins

Gwen, now free of Ralph, began a long roller coaster ride with James E. Burnett. Jimmy, as he was better known, was a short, pint-sized Englishman, with a giant ego and temperament to match. Thirteen years in Quebec and Ontario did little to smooth off the sharp corners carved by his fight for survival.

However, quite surprisingly, James filled the bill for Gwen in so many ways that her friends were not aware of.

Everyone knew of her desire to create and project the movie star image. They also knew of her craving for male attention. Little did they ever dream that she would settle for this short Englishman, with a full blown Napoleonic complex. She, as always, was the center of all the action. He stayed in her shadow, and lived vicariously through her. That seemed to work for him. He was passive about her flirtations because he knew ultimately, she would return to him. Few men would, or could provide for her financially as he did, and still endure her wanderlust. It worked for them. She had the perpetual male admirers she craved and needed, and he rode the coat tails of the endless attention. The neighborhood pubs became their homes away from home. Their bar room brawls became legendary. Patrons argued over which couple held the title, "The Battling B's", the more famous, Humphrey Bogart and Lauren Bacall, or the local team, Jimmy and Gwen Burnett. It was not uncommon for them to start out on a Friday night together and meet again Saturday morning, neither remembering where the other had been the previous night, or with whom.

Now, with James's entrance and Ralph's exit, I began my first transition to a series of different parents. Little did I know just how many of these "parents" would permeate my life. I was just one and a half when Gwen delivered her second child. A baby girl. Unfortunately the newborn developed pneumonia and died within weeks of her birth. Another boy was rumored to have been born but this has never been confirmed. Most likely he was another figment of Gwen's most fertile imagination.

She, for years, delighted in telling all who cared enough to listen that her baby Bobbie was sought after, by the Gerber Baby Food Company to grace the cover of their baby food jars. This myth also was never confirmed. Although personally, I think it quite believable.

Since this period framed an era peppered with lost weekends, many of her exploits will remain just interesting stories. But three major incidents do stand out. Moments in time that, put into motion, became events that profoundly affected many, many other people's lives and created quite a few bends in my journey.

Chapter Four
Three Strikes-You're out

A Foggy Night

The first incident began late on a Friday night as James and Gwen, for a change, headed home together. It was just outside St. Catharines on a gravel road, very early hours of the morning. Fog had shrouded the fields and was slowly creeping across the highway. They were less than a half mile from home, when as usual; they began arguing about who did what to whom at the last bar. It's not known if it was inattention, anger or simply the misty fog that caused James to run the stop sign. Blasting out of the fog, the delivery van slammed into the passenger side of their car. The door caved in, crushing Gwen across the seat and into James. The windshield shattered, showering shards of glass throughout the car. James and Gwen were critically injured. It took over three months of operations and hospital care. Afterwards, came weeks of rehabilitation.

It also created another problem. What to do with little Bobbie? Who would care for him?

That night, Margaret had just returned from seeing a movie when she received a call from the hospital advising her that Gwen had been hospitalized. She was requested to relieve the babysitter and take young Bobbie home. Margaret had just married Johnnie, a wonderful, friendly, caring young man. He was happy for them to take Bobbie. They eventually wanted children of their own, so this could be construed as a trial run.

And so for the next three months I had a guaranteed home. One, incidentally, a little closer to normalcy, than in the past. And so I began my third parental adjustment. But like everything else in my life, it too, was to be short lived. I liked my Aunt Margaret and I hoped my stay would be permanent. Several months passed and James and Gwen eventually mended, at least, physically. I had adapted to the new lifestyle quite well and in my own childish way, hoped I was here to stay. It once again, was not to be. Jim and Gwen had both sought and found new jobs and finally, perhaps reluctantly, presumably at their request, I was returned home to live once more with my Mommy and James.

It was to a new and quieter home than before. Though at three, I was much too young to appreciate it. Unfortunately, the serenity was short lived. New apartment, new neighborhood and ultimately new pubs to check out. The tensions from sky-high hospital bills and very little money, grew and festered, and their need to get away from it, increased. The burgeoning bills eventually led to the decision to move across town and eventually for James to become an insurance salesman. James soon discovered that his forte was not in wooing people to buy his products. His brash, curt, insulting manner did little to augment his paycheck. His boss finally suggested that perhaps James should consider looking for work using his hands. James's caustic retorts to his manager's suggestion ended his insurance career on a rather sour note. A moment in time, that Jimmy over the rest of his life, derived great pleasure in the re-telling.

The economy was slowly beginning to pick up. The war against Germany was over. Japan was rumored to be on the verge of capitulation and the steel mills were hiring all they could recruit. Perhaps, actually working with his hands was the answer. James applied and became a laborer in the smelting mills. For a time, the money was worth the hours and the back-breaking work. But eventually, Jimmy decided that he had to find a better way. Besides, they expected you to show up at work, every morning. Some mornings, hangovers made that an exceedingly difficult if not a completely impossible task. Again, he was faced with another decision regarding his future. While contemplating his next change in his life, Gwen continued her part time job in the local bowling alley. Her personal income paying for a large part of their regular evening libations and additionally the occasional sitter for me.

The Unfaithful Ford

A whole year passed with unending trials and tribulations. James worked in the mill; Gwen worked disinfecting bowling shoes. She eventually became the Bowling Alley manager. And I, well, simply grew a year older. The lack of dissension between them almost allayed the perpetual fear that something surely will eventually happen. This almost normal home life seemed at least momentarily, to promise a brighter future. Then the second major incident occurred.

Late one night, James joined her at work, and together they had closed the bowling alley, cleaned up the cigarette butts and garbage. Signed out the staff and hurried out the back door to the alley. Hopefully, they could make it to the hotel before last call. The usually faithful Ford turned over and over. James swore at the car and Gwen hollered at him for not having taken care of whatever was preventing it from starting. She yelled and angrily said she was not waiting around, she would walk to the hotel. He could walk over later.

She had barely reached the end of the alley when she heard the Ford growl to life. James gunned the engine angrily and raced down the alley to where she was waiting. The roaring engine drowned out whatever she yelled at him as she jumped in. James floored the accelerator and with tires screaming, exploded out into the middle of Geneva Street. Unseen to his left, the last trolley for the night was heading south for the barn. Without warning it rammed into the driver's side, ripping through the fender and shattering the door. Jimmy's body was slammed against Gwen driving both of them through the windshield. The trolley dragged their Ford almost half a city block, till the twisted, smoking wreck finally ground to a screeching halt. James and Gwen were both unconscious. Bystanders couldn't believe anyone had survived the crash. They were rushed to St Catharine's General Hospital, Intensive Care Unit. They somehow survived.

This time Gwen's sister, Margaret was unavailable, since she was eight months pregnant with her first child. Consequently, her sister and her husband Mark were called. Once again I found myself thrust upon the merry-go-round of caretakers, while Mommy and James spent the next seven months of my life, under hospital care. This was to be my fourth parental adjustment. I was not yet five years old.

I turned five living with my Aunt Marion.

Marion & Bobby 3 wks

She was a good woman. As far as I was concerned. She hugged me a lot. Said my prayers with me at night. And spent a lot of time playing with me.

Once again, for a while living with Aunt Marion, I was part of a real family. Then Aunt Marion fell pray to what everyone referred to as 'the sickness". I was too young to understand what exactly the problem was. Sadly, many years later, it was the end result of her alcohol sickness that I became more familiar with.

James and Gwen eventually completed their rehabilitation, but were not able to resume their jobs and most definitively not their lifestyles. The bowling alley job was history, as was their car. The apartment was replaced by a one room flat. There was barely rent money. They didn't want or need to add a five-year-old little boy to their woes. There weren't any more sisters to pawn him off on. Finally, they turned to welfare for help. The surprising help came in the form of another move for me.

Mother Scholastica

Mother Scholastica

St Marjorie's Convent in St. Catharines ran an orphanage for homeless and battered children. The large gray stone building backed up to the remnants of a once beautiful cemetery. The care of it had long ago stopped. Large elms bordered the home on the right and the left faced Thorold Boulevard. As ominous as it was from the outside, the inside, with its maze like corridors and grey shadows crisscrossing in a frightening array, left me pining for my life with any of my past "parents".

Jim Burnett convinced the sisters to take me off their hands. It was supposed to be what was best for me. Ironically, at this point in my young life, I had worked my way through four sets of family caretakers and now my fifth caretaker was to be a very large black robed Nun called Mother Scholastica.

At five years old, I didn't even know what a Nun was. But, I knew I was no longer being cared for by family. But the Mother Scholastica did take good care of me. Eventually, I appreciated having the Nuns for my family. Actually, I was happy to have anyone for a family.

Unfortunately, before my sixth birthday, Gwen was advised by the Convent, that they were not in a position to provide free room and board for children, whose parents were in a financial position to assume that responsibility.

Mother Scholastica said she would pray for me. I soon found out that meant I was going home. Only I had no idea where home was or who with.

Gwen and James moved into a small flat on the same street, where her sister Marion lived. James hadn't been rehired by the mill and Gwen couldn't find any available or suitable employment. Eventually, James was forced to take menial jobs just to pay for rent and food. Marion and her husband Johnny had loaned them as much money as they could whenever they could. They baby-sat me when necessary. They did all they could to help out. Although the economy was on the upswing, James and Gwen didn't seem to be able to capitalize and things were about to worsen.

Bobbie's Pennies

Happier Days

Late one night James and Gwen managed to scrounge up enough change to buy a couple of glasses of ale at the Leonard pub. Marion wasn't available to baby-sit, so I was dragged along. I was left in the hallway sitting on a bench to wait, while they drank beer and pretended that they didn't have a care in the world. James physically planting me on the bench and stern warning not to get off certainly assured me that I best not wander the lobby.

It was evidently still early and the after work crowd had not yet begun to fill the empty corners. The late afternoon drinkers were finally giving up their seats and making their way to the doors. The hotel lobby smelled of stale beer and cigarette smoke. Bare concrete bled through the permanently stained tiles, carving even deeper the trails laid down by the legions passing from the front desk to their sheltered cubicles.

Tired travelers upstairs made all their necessary telephone calls then washed up and put on their last clean shirt before heading back through the lobby, in search of either food or fun or both.

Sitting in the lobby on the heavy wooden bench against the wall, I was unaware of the history surrounding me. I was also unaware that the people coming and going in front of me were equally oblivious and unmindful of the hotel's past and or me. I knew nothing of why these people were laughing or why they were talking so loud. I did know that they smelled of beer and cigarettes. But, why were people I didn't know, smiling at me and pointing? Why were they looking around? Were they looking for my Mommy? Was it my new blue cap? I took off the cap and examined it. Perhaps it looked funny. Maybe it was dirty. No, it appeared all right. I turned it over; it was clean on the inside too. A man and lady stopped and watched me examining the inside. I looked up at them wonderingly. Then it happened.

They dropped three coins in my hat, patted me on the head and walked across the lobby, casting a sad wave, as they disappeared through the big doors. I looked down and counted, one, two, and three. Three shiny pennies. I was not yet six years old and had already made my first monies. I couldn't wait to tell Mommy. I ran to the edge of the doorway into the big room and waved my arms till I caught Mommy's attention. She motioned James to check out the problem. His scowl scared me as he approached, but I told him of the pennies I had collected, and he was all smiles.

He sent me back, cap in hand, to raise another two pennies, which incidentally, added to the others, was the required amount for another glass of beer. I was pleased that I was able to make him so happy. It was probably the last and only time I was able.

In the dimness of the hallway, I found the shine of the pennies intriguing. They seemed to promise me that something special was in store for me. They made me feel good.

Later that evening, James's friend Michael, came from the Men's side and joined them at their table. He laughed as James told him of my panhandling experience, but he had even more exciting news. Vineland area apparently had a winery undergoing extensive renovations, and they needed painters male and female. James reasoned that anybody could wield a brush.

A Truck, a Train and Wine Bottles

Later that evening, back at the house, Gwen pleaded for Marion to once more take care of me. Just for a few weeks till they got back on their feet. Aunt Marion and Uncle Johnny reluctantly agreed. They reminded James again, that this baby sitting job was only for a couple of weeks. Marion helped them pack their few belongings. Early the next morning they bid Marion and Johnny and me goodbye and hopped the trolley, heading across town to the end of the line. A short trek brought them to shoulder of the main highway. Hitch-hiking with a beautiful redhead was a cakewalk. Within minutes a truck loaded with wine bottles, headed for the wineries in the Vineland area pulled over.

They reveled in their good luck. Sitting beside the driver was two servicemen in uniform. The driver motioned them to go to the rear of the truck. James and Gwen ran to the back and climbed up to join another serviceman sitting atop the cases of empty wine bottles. Life was beginning to look better. In an hour they would be at the construction site and could start working again. The bottles rattled incessantly as the truck rumbled toward the winery. They read the sign announcing the final turn onto the property.

No one saw or even heard the train over the clattering of empty bottles, as the truck slowly lumbered across the tracks. The engineer never had a chance to blow the whistle or hit the brakes.

The driver and two servicemen were killed instantly. James, Gwen and the third serviceman were all unconscious and barely alive. All three spent weeks in intensive care and the next five months in and out of different hospitals. just trying to survive the multiple operations and enduring the endless days of therapy.

Their nights were filled with pain and fears. Pains of trying to rebuild their broken bodies and fears about their future. No jobs, no money, no home.

And, oh yes, what about Bobbie? Just another bump in the road.

Seems Marion and Johnny had just inherited an additional problem. They needed to find a new home for me!

Chapter Five
Uncle Leon & Aunt Dorothy

Merritton

If you take a number 2 bus out of St. Catharines, the one, with a sign in the window that says Thorold Road, you will travel to and through a small town called Merritton. Today it's no longer there. It was eventually annexed by St. Catharines.

But in the thirties, it was quite typical of its era. A population of less than eight hundred people enjoyed quiet, urban lifestyles. The town square containing an elevated band shell was the favorite Saturday night choice. Townspeople gathered to listen and applaud the local band. Park benches quickly filled and soon became surrounded by blankets covering all available grass. Young children ran helter skelter, totally unsupervised. Teenagers tried to look bored with the music, as they inched their way closer to the band shell. Sing along tunes filled the night air. The old men smoked fat aromatic cigars and the ladies wore hats or scarves, bright red lipstick and rouge dabbed on high cheeks. Young boys wore knickers with patches on the knees. Little girls wore frilly dresses and Mary Jane shoes. It was a much simpler time. Across from the park, even the town hall steps were filled with ardent listeners. There weren't any movie theaters, shopping malls or bright lights or traffic. Just people who knew each other. People who grew up with each other. People who cared about each other. They talked about who was married last week. And the local fire engine, almost not starting in time to extinguish the grass fire started by those "you know who" boys. Plans for the church supper at St. John's Anglican Church were discussed and finalized. But for most, the greatest joy of all was to lie back on the sweet, green grass and spot the first stars to shine through the gray evening haze.

This was how the Rapsey family spent their Saturday nights. Walter and Ada Rapsey. They bought a yellow brick home on Almond Street, shortly after they were married. Walter worked at the paper mill, just up the hill on the west side of town. Their first child, Dorothy was followed quickly by a son, Dalton, another daughter Marjorie and a few years later, another son, Tom.

Dorothy Rapsey

Dorothy Rapsey

Dorothy, or Dodo, as her friends called her, graduated high school and parlayed a part time job at A & P grocery stores, into a full time cashier's position. She was an attractive, intelligent, and socially outgoing young girl. Seldom dated but had lots of offers. She was young and quite selective about whom she would date.

It was on a Thursday afternoon, about four o'clock. The traffic in the A & P grocery store was slow. She was checking prices and punching them in to the cash register, when she glanced at the customer, next in line. He was tall, almost six feet. He was handsome. He had dark hair, almost black, impeccably combed, the depth of his part cutting a white groove from front to back. His clothes expensive and immaculate. His eyes sparkled and his white teeth glistened as he broke into a smile. Leon's approving smile belied his perceived confidence. When he pushed his few items in front of her, she blushed and giggled like a schoolgirl. She felt downright giddy. Then he spoke. She thought he sounded just like Maurice Chevalier. His French accent was intoxicating. "Hello", he said, "you're very pretty". She didn't respond. He smiled even more and asked, "would you like to go out for coffee some time"? She turned back to the register and regained her composure and demurely replied that she didn't date strangers. But this one time, she did and less than a year later she became Mrs. Leon Perras, sister-in-law to Ralph Perras. They were my Aunt Dorothy and Uncle Leon.

Leon Perras

Leon Albert Perras

Leon and his brothers had sought careers in all different directions. Most served a term in the mills, before branching out and following other interests.

Marcel became a store keeper, owning his own store in St. Catharines till he retired. My Aunt Lucille was the smallest, feistiest, and undoubtedly, the most beautiful of the Perras wives. She and Uncle Marcel always treated me special. Always had time for me.

Uncle John and Aunt Helen raised a vibrant family of eight. Their roadside restaurant and gas station kept them and any kids over three feet tall, very, very busy. Uncle John ruled his family much in the style that Grandpa Perras ruled his boys.

Uncle Albert and Aunt Sue moved to Sault St Marie and I remember little of them.

Ralph continued to be the outsider.

But Leon was different. Leon had his future already planned. He most definitely would not be poor. He would become successful and hopefully important. That was a given. His hopes to marry well and have a family were relegated to phase two. Leon's plans seemed to fit well with Dorothy's dream future.

She had descended from a family of factory workers. He could be her way out of mediocrity, and up the social ladder. Leon had spent eight years in an Ottawa public school and felt that was enough education for him. He quit when he turned fourteen and spent several years searching for the right career move. As a young man, he had a way with the girls, and became a most popular man among the guys. Following Leon, you were able to coat-tail on his charm and popularity and share in his social life. Although he hadn't as yet, attained any position financially, he always seemed to have money to spend when the occasion called for it.

Mister Charm as he enjoyed being referred to also became known as Mister big-shot. Not quite as appealing. He was truly a megalomaniac in the making. Part of his positive charm was from his belief in what he could and would do in life.

Like most entrepreneurs, he knew and accepted the fact that he would step on many people in his quest for riches. And with this attitude he began his climb.

As a small time boxer, part time lumberjack, construction worker and steel mill laborer, he strived to rise above the norm. It took only a short period until he, like his brothers found out that with only a limited command of English, he was virtually without a future. He knew he must become fluent in English if he were to achieve his ambitions. Later in life his command was far above the average university graduate. He may have had only an eighth grade education, but his English speaking and writing far exceeded college level. This became preponderant to his later successes in life. Blue collar jobs were a temporary albatross. The white collar, high roller, lifestyle became his sole aspiration.

Co-incidentally and unknown to each other, Leon and James Burnett both chose the London Life Insurance Company as their choice destiny. However, unlike Burnett, Leon enjoyed the challenges presented by the insurance industry. He found it easy to convince people of their need for family protection. Selling insurance afforded him the opportunity to earn enough money to buy the latest clothing fashions. He could buy an almost new car. But perhaps even more importantly, it opened avenues to management.

This was definitely his destiny. After long days collecting insurance premiums, in the field, he would return home to the dining room table and switch from studying insurance to studying English and back to insurance. For several years he relentlessly pursued his education.

He was eventually appointed assistant sales manager, followed by Branch Manager and in the fifties he was appointed the Superintendent of Agencies. Still a young man, he had his eye on upper level management. But after a few years as Superintendent, he found to his dismay and anger that he had reached and crashed into his glass ceiling. Without a College degree he could go no further.

Chapter Six
New Parents Again

The 6 Year Old Hand-off

Though the war years were turbulent and troubled, they were also in some ways, rather beneficial. The war itself brought too much sadness and heartbreak. Brothers and sisters, husbands and wives were separated, some never to return.

Among the lucky ones was Dorothy's brother Dalton, who served his time overseas, met his wife Muriel in England, and brought her home with him. Ralph and Gwen's sister Marion after serving in the WACs also returned.

On the home front, the mills were operating at capacity. With the diminished population to draw from, work was readily available to those who wanted it. It was the beginning of a new decade with a great future, when Leon asked Dorothy to marry him. He had left the steel mill grime behind and found a white collar occupation, with the capacity to allow him to realize his ambitions. His first major acquisition was a small red brick house, number 7

Taylor Avenue in St. Catharines. Lucky number 7. He was ready for the next item on his agenda. It was time to start his family. But nature just wasn't co-operating. Dorothy couldn't seem to get pregnant.

Meanwhile, Marion and Johnny knew they couldn't continue to care for me and so had to explore caretaker options. Gwen's family had carried the burden of a young boy, off and on for five years. They were now too busy with their own families to take on another year of Bobbie. James didn't have any family, so that left no one to turn to. It appeared that the only possibility might be Ralph's family.

All the married brothers were well into their own families. Only Leon and Albert Junior hadn't any children yet. Uncle Albert and Aunt Sue lived hundreds of miles away and no one knew how to reach them.

Fortunately, Ralph provided Marion with Leon's St.Catharines address. It turned out to be a blessing for all. Leon and Dorothy were still trying to have children. Although a six -year old was somewhat older than they had planned on, they agreed to take care of him, until James and Gwen had recovered physically and hopefully financially. Uncle Leon and Aunt Dorothy loved me and I loved them in return. It was a perfect home setting. I finally had a family of my own and a home too. A little more than a year had passed and one day Gwen came to visit me with Dorothy and Leon. They sat me down and told me that I would be living with Uncle Leon from now on. I didn't fully understand, except I was happy to hear that I wasn't going to be uprooted and moved again. Even at six years old I appreciated that I had a sense of permanency and I also had made many new friends. I really wouldn't miss my Mommy that much, since I really hadn't spent that much time with her, up until now. Interestingly, I found out years later, from Gwen, that when she and James had sufficiently recuperated, they arranged a visit with Leon and Dorothy. Gwen's story was that my Aunt and Uncle wanted to be paid for the period of time they cared for me and said if Gwen and Jim couldn't pay, they would have to let them adopt me. Leon and Dorothy's story was that Gwen and James really didn't have the time or room for a kid in their lifestyles, and literally pleaded with them to take me off their hands. The truth has never been established and evidently, never will. Ultimately, it became a mixed blessing for me, that they agreed and Aunt Dorothy became Mommy and Uncle Leon became Daddy. Daddy, now that was a term I hadn't used very much!

Short Time Happy

During my stay at 7 Taylor Street in St Catharines, I enjoyed our two Pekinese dogs and the company of two brothers and their sister who lived next door, and a back yard with lots of grass to play on. I was a very happy little boy.

Shortly after my adoption, we moved to Verdun, Quebec. We lived in a nice neighborhood, near the location of my first school. Dorothy enrolled me and very soon was pleased that I was learning to speak French. She assumed that I was picking it up from my new friends. Turns out that she had enrolled me in a French school and everyone spoke French.

She overcame her embarrassment enough to quickly re-enroll me in an English school. Returning home, after my first day at the new school, Dorothy said to me, "What is your teacher's name" I replied "yes, that's right" She chided me for being saucy. She asked me again and received the same response. I looked up at her and said, "What is my teacher's name". "Bobbie, she said clearly annoyed, don't be flippant"! "What is your teacher's name?" "Mommy", I said, near to tears, "What is my teacher's name". Angrily, she sent me to my room, not to come out until I would give her a civil answer. Leon came home shortly and asked where I was. Dorothy told him of my mocking her. He went to my bedroom and shortly emerged laughing, holding me by the hand. Dorothy, reluctantly smiled when he explained that my teacher's name was Mrs. Watt.

After a period in Quebec, we returned to Ontario. I had enjoyed my new parents for almost two years. Life was good. Leon's career was flourishing, we lived well above average and the world was once again turning in well greased grooves.

Dark clouds however, began to accumulate on the horizon. Dorothy had started feeling poorly. Nothing serious, just sort of run down. She just couldn't seem to get the energy to do the everyday chores. It was decided to take her to the doctor for a routine check up. He examined her and ordered a series of tests.

The results were a precursor of things to come. My new Mommy had Tuberculosis! They were advised that the only recognized treatment for Tuberculosis was 24 hour a day rest in a Sanitarium. She was to spend the next four years thus confined. Leon Perras, the budding financier, was about to become a single father. This was definitely not in his game plan. A boy with a woman to look after him was easy, but a boy that Leon alone must care for, was a serious problem. Leon had no intentions of becoming a baby sitter. It appeared that I was heading for another set of parents.

Chapter Seven
Another New Start

My Merritton Home

As noted previously, the Wright side of the family had served their time as surrogate parents and all the Perras brothers had their own, ever increasing families, so it became apparent that Dorothy's family may be the answer. But Dorothy's brother Tom was only nineteen and her sister Marjorie was as yet unmarried and her other brother Dalton had just returned from the war, with his English bride, Muriel. He was well on the way to starting his own family. It seemed to Leon that the only answer was Dorothy's parents Walter and Ada Rapsey.

The Rapseys

Perhaps it was trauma or just the passage of time, but my memories of the transition from my new home with my new Mommy and Daddy, to my "Grandma and Grandpa" Rapsey's house in Merritton, is, at best sketchy. I was about seven, I believe, and was already in the second grade. I had already been in so many homes, that I didn't take any particular interest in my new surroundings, since I felt it would only be another footnote in my ever-increasing list of residences. Little did I suspect that my time with the Rapsey's would be the only time in my life when I felt I was a part of "my" family.

The Rapsey house was on a non-descript street in a small non-descript town. The main street was only a three minutes walk away, and, in less than fifteen minutes, you could be in the country. St Catharines was a twenty minute bus ride and the Welland Canal was a thirty minute bike ride. Their house was a two story yellow brick, with a wide veranda stretching across the front. Three wide wooden steps led to the short sidewalk to the street.

Entering the front door, you were in a wonderful old wood, hand crafted foyer. An aged polished wood staircase led to a landing half way up the stairs. In the soft filtered light from the high ornate window the stairs glistened beneath the polished handrails. Straight ahead from the front door led to the kitchen, or a sharp left turn took you to the basement. To the right was the parlor. It seemed so dark and mysterious.

The outstanding feature of the small room was the large player piano. Dark polished oak, with sliding doors, behind which hid the apparatus that housed the player piano rolls. When the rolls were threaded, one could pull out a double set of floor pedals and by pumping furiously, force air through the paper roll perforations and produce piano music. It was all quite magical. It was on this instrument that some years later I picked out my first Boogie Woogie and began a life long love of the keyboard. It also became rather instrumental in altering the course of my life in a few surprising turns.

Past the piano and on the other side of the parlor were heavy dark oak, double pocketed doors leading into the living room. These doors were always kept tightly shut. The parlor was off limits to a young seven year old.

The living room next to the big doors was the evening entertainment room. Grandpa's reading chair and grandma's knitting chair sat opposite the radio.

The bullet radio, so called because it resembled a large bullet, sat on four slender legs. With just the right amount of wiggle room a young man, laying on his back, could slide under and stare up at the underside of the radio while conjuring up the images of the Lone Ranger, Fibber McGee and Molly, The Shadow, Crime Busters and of course the adult's favorite, Lux Family Theater.

The far side of the room had a large bay window that extended out from the side of the house, which afforded a panoramic view of Grandma's side yard.

The large, bright kitchen had a chrome-trimmed wood-burning stove. A whistling kettle was always kept on top, so that tea could be served at a moment's notice. Wood was kept in sturdy box beside the stove. When someone noticed that the kitchen was a tad cool, one flipped open the lid and another small log was dropped in. Soon the room was warm again. The inside wall was filled with dishes and other paraphernalia that a young boy had little interest in. But the drawers beneath the counter were especially interesting. The bottom one was called the junk drawer. It eventually became, Bobbie's Treasure Drawer. On rainy days, I would delight in "cleaning it out" for Grandma. Tools, shoe polish, screws, nails, rags and several items that I never did figure out what they were. And wonderful, unidentifiable smells. It was a cornucopia of treasures for a curious lad. When Grandma baked and I sorted the junk drawer, the combination of the smells overwhelmed the olfactory senses. Some scents stay in your memory for ever.

Off to the corner of the kitchen was a doorway leading to a staircase. Half way up you reached the same landing that you could also reach, from the front door. I found it great fun to run up the kitchen stairs and then down the front stairs, around the hall and back up the kitchen stairs again. I learned very quickly to enjoy this sport only when Grandma was out of the house.

Walking up the stairs from the kitchen to the half landing, to your right you looked down upon the driveway between the houses. Turn left and you climbed six more steps to the second floor hallway. First door on the right belonged to Grandma's youngest son Tom. He was about thirteen years older than I and something of a mystery to me, since I very seldom ever saw him. He was a carpenter, when he worked, which seemed infrequent. Generally, he was either working or out with his friends at the corner hotel. I do remember on occasion though, he would give me a quarter and a small tin pail, and send me to the hotel to fetch him a bucket of beer. The return trip without any spilled netted me a nickel tip. Enough for one of those giant two scoop ice cream cones.

Mary Dunlop

Across the hall was Mary Dunlop's room. A fine lady teacher who rented a room from Grandma for more years than anyone can remember. She was a very quiet lady and kept pretty much to herself. She taught kindergarten in the public school half a block away. I joined her and Grandma in the kitchen for breakfast every morning. I remember how fascinated I was, as I watched her dissect the poached egg on toast that Grandma prepared for her. The egg was always perfectly cooked, gently placed in the middle of brown toast. Then she would carefully cut the egg north to south three times, then east to west three times. All the while being careful not to allow any egg to fall off the toast and on to the plate. She then with a surgeon's touch spread the egg equally to all the edges of the toast. It delighted me to check her plate when she was finished to see if any had actually touched the china. It never did.

Next to Mary's room at the other end of the hall was Grandma's room. Her window looked out the back over the flower gardens she tended daily. Her dresser was decorated with hand made doilies and perfume and powder containers. Exotic smells wafted from her door as one walked down the hall to the bath. I have, ever since, equated the aroma of sweet perfume and powder with femininity. Forbidden and mysterious. This room along with Mary's room was forbidden territories. I could stand and enjoy the exciting smells of gardenia and lilac and powders, but dared not to enter.

Next to the bathroom on the driveway side was Grandpa's room. Barely big enough for his double bed, it became my room too. An army cot, the canvas kind that folds up for easy transportation, was found and set up between his bed and the wall. Barely room for me to squeeze by, let alone an adult. But it was my bed, and I loved it.

Grandpa Rapsey

Every night Grandpa would get ready for bed by stripping down to his skivvies and getting out the giant bottle of liniment. Grandpa Rapsey had his very own special smell. He was a walking ad for Absorbine Junior. He would proceed by rubbing his shoulders first, then his arms, then thighs, hips and lower back. By the time he got down to his legs the room was filled with this overpowering smell. He said that without his magic elixir, he wouldn't even be able to walk. So while he rubbed, we would talk. And when he finished we would lie in bed and wait for the nine-eighteen train whistle. Each night in the quiet darkness, Grandpa would wait to hear the faint train whistle and then say to no one in particular; there goes the nine-eighteen, right on time. Then he'd touch my arm, and say goodnight and turn over. I lay on my army cot, looking out the window, watching the twinkling of the stars, listening to the train fade in the distance and thought how lucky I was.

Grandpa was in his sixties when I was dropped into his life. His daughter Dorothy was my Aunt; so technically, he wasn't even a direct relative. He had just retired, so he certainly didn't need the responsibility of a young boy. And he was not exactly a healthy man.

He had worked all his life in the paper mill, less than a half mile from his home. His hands and face and neck were brown and spotted. His fingers were arthritic and swollen and misshapen. He walked severely stooped over and winded easily. He enjoyed his gardens and the news on the radio. He loved the neighborhood kids and they all enjoyed him.

Each day as he walked along the railroad tracks to and from work, he would collect railroad warning flares that failed to ignite or only burned part way. Every couple of weeks, on a warm summer evening, I'd beg him to "do the flares". When he consented, I'd round up the kids and we'd gather around the front yard, jostling for best position, till he came out of the garage with a box of red flares. He'd stick the nail end of the flare into the ground and lighted the sulfur at the top. Red flames would spurt out, turning the whole front yard into a magical arena where shadows flickered red, yellow and sometimes blue. We'd all dance like wild Indians, hollering so loud the neighbors peered out to see what the ruckus was all about. Perhaps they merely wanted to enjoy the show.

The White Owl

Grandpa loved his cigars. He smoked only the White Owl brand. But as much as he loved them, Grandma hated them. So Grandpa was relegated to the basement in the winter and the front porch in the summer. After supper every night, when the snow was deep and the night air freezing, Grandpa would slowly make his way down the creaky staircase to the basement. The floor was half concrete and half mud hardened to the consistency of concrete. The rafters were less than six feet high. This was not a problem for either of them since they were both well under the lowest beam.

The basement was a treasure trove of new things. Grandpa's workbench in the corner always contained something he was in the midst of repairing. Grandma took over one whole corner for her washing. And even took to hanging stuff from the rafters to dry when inclement weather necessitated it. But it would have to have been really bad weather, because I recall many a day helping her retrieve frozen laundry from the back clothesline.

In the farthest reaches of the basement was the coal bin and furnace. Beside the furnace, just under the big pipe was Grandpa's stool. This was his smoking stool. He could sit here during inclement weather, open the furnace door and flick the ashes of his cigar onto the flames. Sometimes he would send me a few feet to the bin to bring another shovel full of coal. He'd open the grated door and I'd feel so grown up, dumping the whole load in the furnace and not scattering it all over the floor. Which unfortunately I did on many occasions.

I used to feel so sad that he had to come to the basement to smoke his cigar. I realized years later, that this was not an entirely bad thing. I believe he really did enjoy his sanctuary.

The front veranda stretched across the entire house. It was ground level on the north end and was about eighteen inches high at the south end. This is relevant only because it permitted an entry from the north.

Every summer night Grandpa would sit on the top of the veranda steps. Every night he would meticulously remove the cigar band from his White Owl cigar. He would then fold it in half and slip it between the two slats of the second step up the front veranda. Then he would take his pocket knife and trim the end of the fat cigar. Swirl it around in his mouth, lick the entire length and then with a flourish, strike the wooden match across the stone pillar beside him and hold it exactly one inch below the tip and puff gently till the end glowed fiercely.

Looking out across Almond Street to the houses of neighbors he'd known for thirty years, he savored his smoke. His eyes closed, no doubt remembering the half century he toiled in the paper mill, and probably wondered about the number of tomorrows left.

I on the other hand was intrigued with, and questioned where, all those cigar wrappers went.

The Great Cigar Caper

One fine afternoon, when nothing better presented itself to do, my friend Billy Watson who lived only three doors away, and who was my best friend for several years, and I, decided to initiate a little investigation. We needed to find out what happened to all those cigar wrappers. No one was at home. Grandma and Grandpa had gone to town grocery shopping. It was the perfect time. Carefully, we pulled aside the shrubs that covered and protected the end of the veranda. The one side of the lattice work had worked itself loose over the years and took very little effort to pry it out far enough to allow two eight year-old explorers to crawl through. Billy, about a head shorter than me, crawled through first. We were met with cobwebs and scurrying little objects. Most of this wildlife we had already encountered many times in the outside world, but here in the underworld, under the porch, they took on a most sinister appearance. The ground smelled musty. The basement foundation had unidentifiable growths on it. We peered out to the street from under the beams. We were afraid to breathe; for fear that someone might hear us. Slowly we inched our way further along the damp cool earth, crawling on our bellies till finally we reached our goal. There, out in front of us were the steps. Light shone down through the cracks.

Illuminated in the sun's shaft was "the cone". It was sadly, not the treasure we had hoped for. Instead, it was a ten inch high pile of White Owl cigar wrappers. Hundreds of them! Years of smoking represented by this single pile of folded wrappers. Ever so tenderly, quivering with

55

excitement, we pushed our fingers into the pile. Hoping for the unexpected. The peak toppled over and slid down its side, joining the other wrappers. An unidentifiable bug ran out from the toppled cone. Was that all? Was this the end of our quest?

Sadly, that was it. Nothing more exciting than cobwebs and old cigar wrappers. We crawled back the length of the veranda to the opening and carefully pulled the lattice back in place.

The great cigar caper was a bust! But at least we now knew where all the wrappers went!

Grandma Rapsey
Field Day

Many events happen that change the course of one's life. Some are situations that at the time seem so insignificant and unimportant; one could never image anything ever being affected by it. Still other events that we feel should or could change our lives, amazingly don't have any lasting impact whatsoever. I've never understood if my path in life was ever affected by what started out as the swiped peach episode.

Grandma Rapsey was a wonderful, caring and loving grandmother. She took me in and loved me as her own. She taught me lessons in life, every day. Most of which I wasn't aware of at the time. She taught me to cook. When she made pies, I was given my own handful of dough to roll out and a spoonful of filling. She taught me to knit a scarf, to crochet doilies out of string and to pick sweet peas from her garden.

She also taught me how to become a champion. With

the annual field day coming in less than a month, I was determined to win a blue ribbon. I was entered in the high jump, the broad jump and the hop, skip and jump. I was also in the one hundred yard race. I used to race up and down Almond Street to build up my stamina.

One day Grandma sat me down and asked how serious I was about winning. I told her I wanted a blue ribbon more than anything in the world. She said she would tell me how I could win, but I had to promise to follow her advice, unwaveringly. I eagerly agreed. She went to my closet and pulled out my high cuts. These were my leather winter boots that came up to mid-calf. They were great in the snow, but they were quite heavy. In the summer, they were really, really heavy. Her advice was simple. For the next four weeks, I was to wear them to school every day. And for every event that I practiced, I had to keep them on. I had promised her I'd follow her advice, so I had little choice. I endured the jeers from my friends and classmates. I shed more than a few tears each time I came in last in the practice events. I persevered.

The morning of the Field Day, I laced on my sneakers. The same sneakers that lay in the back of my closet for a long, long month. As soon as I picked them up, I was shocked. You would have thought that they were made of feathers. Throughout field-day, I jumped higher, sprinted faster and leapt longer than I ever dreamed possible.

The newspaper the next day printed my name as the winner of three blue ribbons and two red ones. I won the pole vault and the long jump and finished second in the sprint, high jump and the hop-skip & jump. I was truly the champion. And I owed it all to my Grandma Rapsey.

Chapter Eight
Destiny or Choice

Pliers, Paint & Peaches

Grandma canned fruit every fall and my job was to help her peel, cut, wash and generally do all the time consuming easy jobs. My reward was to share in taste testing the final products. Canned peaches were my favorites. One corner in the basement, Grandpa had set up shelves on which they stored Grandma's preserves. They were piled from floor to ceiling, three deep. Enough for the whole winter. They also looked so inviting to two eight years-olds.

Billy and I weighed the chances of anyone discovering one missing jar of peaches. Confident that the deed would never be discovered, we carefully took a quart of peaches off the shelf. Pulled the two filled ones from behind to the forward slot, effectively covering the void left by our theft. The perfect crime.

To this day, I don't know how she discovered the theft. But she did. And she was angry. Not because of the loss of a quart of peaches. But because I would steal from her and then cover it up. Grandma was angry, and hurt. I was contrite, but in big trouble. I was confined to my room for a whole week.

Grandpa was mister fix-it. If it was broken, he could fix it. He could fix the car, fix the plumbing, and fix the lamps. It didn't matter what it was Grandpa could fix it. He even had an iron shoe last and many boxes of shoe tacks. When the soles wore out, Grandpa could put on new ones. He also had leather shoe trimmings left over. He gave long strands of leather strips to Billie Watson and me. We wove them into long whips attached to a leather wrapped handle, which allowed us to crack the whip and pretend we were Lash Larue of cowboy fame. We even held pieces of paper in our teeth allowing the whippor to snap it out of the whippee's mouth. Hopefully without clipping one's cheek or ear.

Grandpa had an array of hand tools, saws, hammers, pliers, screwdrivers. Like most eight year olds, I loved to take them out in the back yard and build things. One of the most popular endeavors was a soap box scooter. It consisted of an old disassembled pair of roller skates, nailed to a flat board and a vertical handle, hopefully fastened securely enough to withstand the rigors of controlling this speed machine.

Sometimes, I would forget to return his tools to the workbench. If I was lucky, I would find them in the grass, where I'd left them, before he did. Most times, I wasn't so lucky. He was a most patient and understanding grandpa, but when it came to his tools, his patience morphed into anger. When he refused to even talk to me at night before bed, I knew I had really crossed the line. This was big trouble.

Grandpa's garage, behind the house was a treasure chest waiting to be discovered. There were all manner of things stored there. The usual, tires, batteries, old inner tubes, broken bicycle parts, even a large assortment of lumber, so vitally important to our building projects. And there was a large array of paint cans. Must have been fifteen partial gallon cans. Rose, from the bedrooms, gray, from the trim, yellow, from the kitchen, brown, from the back porch, and blue from the front porch.

It was a boring rainy afternoon; Billie and I were rummaging in the garage looking to find something to do, when we discovered all the paint cans. Curious about the actual color of the paint in each can, we decided to use the inside of the double garage doors as a very large canvas. A dab of blue blended with a streak of yellow. Brown added shadows and the rose paint brightened the place up. As we found more and more paint our collage mostly covered the entire surface of both doors. I will never know why we didn't stop to think of the consequences of this un-requested paint job. But we didn't. Certainly, it didn't come as a surprise when the next time Grandpa went to the garage, he came looking for me. Trouble seemed to follow me. Or maybe I went out of my way looking for it. Either way, I was going to pay the price for my indiscretions. As Grandpa so often said, you do the crime, you serve the time.

Shake Hands and Say Goodbye

With my chin low on my chest, visions of punishment running rampant through my brain, I walked purposefully, three doors down and found Billy Watson, my cohort in the crime spree, and lamented my woeful situation. Billy, of course agreed with me. I hadn't done anything so terribly wrong. The peaches were after all, just one jar, of many, and the tools could certainly be cleaned of the rust. And the garage? Well, it needed painting anyway.

There were few if any outward signs indicating the sequence of events about to unfold. Perhaps modern day psychology might have been able to predict a mixed up child's rationalizations. But in the nineteen forties, some things were beyond comprehension.

For whatever reasons, I had decided that my life was useless. I couldn't seem to keep parents. I never knew when I would be moving again. I felt I was never going to have a regular family. Everyone else had their Mom and Dad. I had a Grandma and Grandpa. And now, I had caused much hurt and even anger for the only two people that seemed to genuinely care about me. Now it seemed inevitable that I was going to have to move again. When you're barely eight years old and permanency has never been a regular part of your life, maybe you subconsciously think that this time, too, it's going to end as did all the other relationships. Perhaps you feel it would be better to at least have control of your own destiny. That may be giving an eight-year old far too much credit. But for some totally unfathomable reason, I decided that I had to do something drastic.

Through the eyes of an adult, what ensued was totally illogical. But to a mixed up child, I felt the answer was obvious. I concocted a plan which I laid out to Billy. I had him swear to secrecy. Trying to appear casual, we walked the steps up to Grandpa's bedroom. After securing the door we found a small scrap of paper. With a freshly sharpened pencil stub, I scribbled the words, "Dear Mr. Main"; he was the owner and druggist at Main's Drug Store. "Please give Bobbie some sleeping pills for me, because I haven't been able to sleep". Signed, "Ada Rapsey". It was a simple plan. Mr. Main, who knew me well, and Grandma for a lifetime, handed over a vial containing 24 pills. He said he hoped these would help her to sleep.

I smiled and said nothing. By now Billie was getting concerned that I was actually serious. I assured him that I was. We went home and quietly climbed the back staircase leading to the hall bathroom.

It was painted a light blue with white ceramic fixtures. One wall had a cabinet containing all manner of jars and vials. The giant iron tub was against the other wall. Beside the toilet was a window that looked out over the back yard. The winter storm windows were still on. Grandpa hadn't gotten around to removing them yet. They were the types that were custom made to fit each window. Across the bottom, in order to let in some air, one had to lift a wooden slat that exposed four half dollar sized holes. Lifting this slat would allow a small amount of air to circulate. After a solemn goodbye and a sincere but drawn out handshaking with Billie, I filled a glass with water and proceeded to take all twenty-four pills. When I finished, I poked the empty vial out one of the little portholes and watched as it rolled down the back porch roof settling in the eave's trough. As it rolled and tumbled down the shingles, I thought to myself how it seemed to parallel my short journey through life. Deep musings for one so young.

Once again I assured Billie that this would make a lot of people happy. He knew about all my different homes and caretakers. He knew better than anyone how I felt. Even so, he was rather reluctant about renewing his vow not to divulge to anyone what I had done.

We said goodbye one last time and he sneaked down the back stairs and darted out to the back lane, heading home. No doubt wondering what's going to happen next. I went into my Grandpa's room, combed my hair, took off my glasses and lay down on my back in the middle of Grandpa's bed, and waited for the end. My lids got heavy and I felt my eyes slowly close. Eventually I succumbed to a deep, deep sleep.

How Could You Do This To Me?

Five o'clock arrived and it was time for supper. Grandma called out the back door for me to come in. When I didn't come running, she called upstairs. Concerned that I may have been ill and was lying down, she sent her son Tom to check on me. Tom evidently couldn't wake me. He returned downstairs and informed Grandma.

The next happenings were all a blur as I drifted in and out of consciousness. I can remember Tom carrying me, over his shoulder, and down the front stairs to the foyer. I remember Billy standing by the door, sobbing uncontrollably. People were yelling at each other. I was draped over Tom's shoulder. Billy's wail pierced through everyone's shouting. "It's not my fault. I didn't think he would do it. It's not my fault."

I vaguely remember the cab, or car ride to the hospital. I know I was in the back seat and I must have fallen to the floor because I remember lying across the hump in the middle of the floor... I remember a tube going down my throat, and many, many people all around. I recall when I finally awoke, half walking and half being dragged down hospital corridors with a nurse on either side, supporting me, and forcing me to drink copious amounts of black coffee. At some point they allowed me to return to bed. A welcome change from being dragged up and down the halls. I wanted only to crawl under the sheets, anybody's sheets and go to sleep. Mercifully they finally left me alone and I quickly drifted back into that security blanket of sleep. I don't know how long it lasted, but I was violently awakened from my solitude by my adopted mother, Dorothy, slapping my face. They had brought her directly from the sanitarium to the hospital. She was told to keep me awake as long as possible. She slapped my face on the left side then right side, then left side then right side. Each slap accompanied by the hysterical lament, "Bobbie, how could you do this to me? How could you do this to me?" Even in my drug-induced stupor, I seriously questioned her priorities. What was she talking about, how could I do this to her? What did she mean? I was the one being slapped and I couldn't understand why. What had I done so wrong that necessitated physically slapping me? All I wanted to do was go back to sleep and never wake up. Sadly, my failed endeavor to solve all my problems only compounded them for me and unfortunately, created a world of hurt for those who loved me.

Evidently the adults decided that the incident never happened and it was never to be mentioned again. It never was. Not until almost a decade later when Dorothy screamed at me while administering one of her special brands of punishment; "I wish you had died, you're the cause of all our problems!"

Chapter Nine
Innocence Lost

A Period of Exploration

1946 was a year of frustrations and fears. Exploring freedoms that came naturally with age and freedoms that came with living in a new lifestyle. My new grandparents hadn't had on-the-job parenting for at least twenty-five years. In some aspects they were probably too strict and in others, far too lax. I went to bed each night wondering how long this location was good for. Would my new Mother and Father ever really come back for me or would they to palm me off on someone else as my first Mother had so willingly done, so many times? Did my Grandma and Grandpa resent my intrusion into their lives? So many questions, so few answers.

After the visit at the hospital, Dorothy and Leon left. She returned to the Sanitarium, and he to his pursuits. I returned home to the Rapsey's. Very little was ever discussed and I actually never really thought much about it. I was like a little puppy. I had a lot of exploring to do and it was a big exciting world out there. I had learned early in life, let the yesterdays go and live only for the new tomorrows.

Billie and I had become as Grandma used to say, "Thicker than thieves". Next door to our house was the preacher's house. We usually walked a wide berth around his place. Him being close to God and all. Next was the Brown house. Home to Davy and his older brother Dick. Dick was already a teenager. He lived in a different world from ours. But occasionally he gifted us with his presence and wisdom. He had left the sneaker world and was fashionably correct in slacks and shiny loafers. We saw little of Dick, which was fine with us. But his younger brother was to become an integral part of the nefarious threesome. We added Davy Brown to our little band and we were complete. The three musketeers. A union that we thought would last through eternity. We played cowboys with B B guns, bow and arrows and whips, like Lash Larue. We climbed cherry trees, swiped apples and watermelons. We found discarded pop bottles, which we cashed in for ice cream mallow rolls. We walked to nearby woods and watched deer and foxes run free.

We stained our shirts with blueberries and our fingers ran red with wild strawberries. We hiked through valleys that had not yet been discovered. We found caves that probably were used to shelter bears. We tasted the sweet summer raindrops and felt the warm sun caress our shirtless bodies. We ran through creeks and swam in the ponds. We watched the modern marvel; the great draw bridge lift high in the sky allowing giant ships to pass under as they forged their way down the Welland Canal. After the ships passed we scrambled up the rocky slope and ran across the bridge and did some high dives into the canal.

It was a summer for discovery. It was the summer we discovered girls. It was also the summer we discovered the grand piano farmhouse.

The Piano

It was early Saturday morning when Billy, Davy and I set out for a day's adventure. We'd decided to ride our bikes all the way to Thorold Road and leave them beside the canal. We often talked about what might be in the great wooded area beyond the locks and decided that today would be the day we found out. The woods were thick as far as the eye could see. It was a magical area that no one until this day had ever explored. We had our nickel bottle of coke and our peanut butter sandwiches and Billy even had some of his Nana's chocolate chip cookies. I had a long seven foot piece of rope, in case we needed to tie up any bad guys, and my Uncle Dalton's hunting knife, presumably for protection. Davy and Billy had their Cub Scout hatchets and a compass. We set out with high hopes and great expectations. By mid morning we had found a dead rabbit, a live deer and an old shack overgrown with ivy. Not too exciting for three adventurers. It was lunchtime and time for a pow-wow.

Do we keep going or call it quits? Billy, always the curious one insisted that just over the next hill would be the adventure we were searching for. Davy, somewhat reluctantly, agreed to go just a little further before making the final decision. As we breathlessly reached the top of the hill, we were awed by the valley that spread out before us. As big as all of Merritton. But without any buildings. It was vast and it was beautiful, but nothing worth investigating. We decided we should head for home, when Billy spied something shiny reflecting from deep in the heart of the valley. We speculated on what it might be. A lost temple, a golden statue, or even a silver vein in the hillside. All or any, were worth checking out. Off we went charging down the hillside on invisible horses. As we drew closer, it became clear that our object was not as magical as we'd imagined. It was an old large deserted farmhouse. Obviously deserted for many, many years. All the glass was broken. Window frames had been wrenched out. Doors were lying across the veranda. Vines had taken over most of the outside walls. Billy and Davy scouted the backside as I checked out the front perimeter. The house had once been a magnificent home to someone. It towered three stories high, including the small window in the attic. We discovered a rear entrance to a basement at the bottom of a dank, musty stairway. A veranda circled the entire house. The railings and banisters long since destroyed and ultimately deteriorated into kindling.

Upon our scouts' return, we decided to risk exploring the interior. Across from the gaping hole that once contained the stately front door, was a hallway on the left, leading to the back of the house, and a staircase on the right, leading to the second floor landing. In the back of the house was the kitchen. The sink still had the old iron pump attached to a long ago dried up well. Remains of a table lay in pieces against the far wall. The back wall housed a staircase that obviously was the interior access to the basement. We'd explore that later. Billy was already upstairs hollering. The landing at the top of the stairs opened to what had apparently been a sitting room of some sort. Maybe an entertainment area. Because occupying the center of the room was the treasure of the day.

A piano. Not one like we had ever seen. This was once a magnificent grand piano. It apparently once had a lift up top, which had been ripped off. One of its three legs had been severely chopped. Most all the strings had been broken and Davy found that if he chopped the remaining strings with his hatchet, they would make wild sounds. With my knife I tried to pick out a tune. We entertained ourselves with this endeavor, till Billy tired of it and attempted to finish the chopping job someone had started on the leg. But it proved to require far more effort than he wanted to expend.

I don't remember what precipitated what happened next. It may have been, as we were peering down through the massive hole in the middle of the floor, to the living room, below. It may have been the ease with which Billy found he could chop through the rotted flooring. Whatever the reason, we began chopping through the floor in a crude circle around the grand piano. As piece by piece gave way to our vicious destruction, we made certain to be back and away as each piece fell.

The original plan to chop a circle around the piano had given way to a less industrious one. Make the existing hole big enough and we could push the piano into it. In retrospect, it was a rather stupid plan, even for three nine year olds. Sort of like sitting on a branch and then cutting it off. Fortunately for us, as we pushed the remains of the instrument across the floor, heading it into the big void, the floor started to creak and then began to slope precariously downward. We scrambled backwards to the edge of the room as the piano made its final journey into the ever widening crevice. The thunderous crash was deafening. Our adrenalin was flowing. Our hearts were pounding in our ears. And the shaking was almost uncontrollable.

Slowly as the dust began to settle, the laughter and screams began. It was awesome. We crawled on hands and knees back to the stairs and raced downstairs to see the end result. When we reached the main floor we cautiously peeked into the living room. It wasn't there! Instead, was a gaping hole in the center of the floor. One storey below, the piano lay embedded in the middle of the muddy basement floor. We raced through the kitchen and down the back steps. Silently standing beside the piano, we looked up through the remains of two floors; we felt we truly had our adventure. One we could tell our grand kids about. But most definitely not our parents.

Girls Aren't All That Bad

Billie was most knowledgeable about girls, since he had an older sister and was privy to all sorts of girl facts. Davy and I had to rely on him for most of our education. Some times education comes from the most unlikely sources.

Late in the summer 1946 we watched as new people moved into the house at the end of our street. It had been vacant for as long as we could remember. It was even rumored to have been haunted. The three of us were saddened to see people moving in. Out the back yard next to the back lane was an old chicken coop. It was the perfect hideout for our cowboy games. The roof was just high enough that one could climb upon it and when shot dead or wounded, effect a magnificent fall, rolling to the low end and landing in a sprawled heap in the tall grass. The coup windows had been covered with plastic. Most were broken and torn, but provided good cover for the gun battles. A chicken wire cage at the far end created a ready made jail provided the prisoner didn't lean too heavily against it. We never thought for a moment that someone we didn't know would actually buy the place.

Jerry Reid and his twin sisters sat on the curb and watched as their family's furniture was carried in. Billie and I sat down beside him and asked if his dad was going to tear down the chicken coop. Jerry didn't even know he had a chicken coop. Whooping and hollering we dragged him out back and showed him our hideout. His younger sisters tagged along. At eight years old, they were just kids, so we allowed them to stand aside while we older guys, at nine and nine and a half, filled Jerry in on the rules of the musketeers. As we told of our exploits, each of us stole furtive glances at Jerry's twins. This was totally new. No one at school was a twin.

And we had a full set right here on our street. We were some kind of celebrities. Later that night Billie and I sat high in the hay loft in the barn behind Billie's house and in hushed tones discussed, "the twins". We both agreed that girls were a pain and we couldn't care less. But we managed to talk about those two pains, till darkness fell. The Reid family promised to be an exciting addition to our territory.

Don't Touch & Don't Lick

Early fall dissolved almost magically into a cold winter and along with sledding, toboggans and makeshift skis we discovered a new past time. The streets of Merritton were not ploughed as were the big city streets. They were left alone till sufficient cars ploughed through them to make a trail. We noticed that as the cars rounded the corner they would slow down, almost coming to a stop. A new game was about to be born. Before the car pulled away, we would hunker down and grab the back bumper. In a full squat we could "power ski" the length of the street, till the car slowed down for another corner. We would then let go before the corner and slide to a stop, hopefully before running into the back of the car. It was great fun, and it became quite a mystery for my grandma. I seemed to lose an inordinate number of mittens. Damp mittens seemed to have a propensity for freezing on metal bumpers. It was eerie the next day to see cars driving by with somebody's mittens frozen to the bumper.

Main's Drugs Store owned by Mr. Main and located on Main Street had a vacant lot next door. It had an iron railing around it. Probably to keep people like Billie and his Musketeers out.

It was on this rail that one frosty Saturday morning, Billie decided to prove either the credibility or the implausibility of the warnings we had all heard so many times. After a frantic run into the drugstore hollering for help, I sheepishly watched as Mr. Main and several onlookers were enjoying Billy's predicament, as warm water was being poured over the connected tongue. Truism proven.

Some adventures were not so easily concluded with a simple glass of warm water.

Grandma's back porch was high off the ground which allowed Grandpa to install a twenty foot steel pole at the end of the property. Attach a couple of wheel pulleys at each end and Grandma had a long very high clothes line. Over the years, mainly because of a lack of protective paint, the steel pole became quite rusted. About four feet from the ground a steel spike protruded about four inches out from the pole. We would use this spike as a first step on the way to shinnying to the top. Once we achieved the apex, we slid back down to earth, basically destroying our T-shirts in the process. The game became more intense as each climber challenged the others to make the fastest trip from top to bottom. Rust chips flew everywhere as we slid down the steel on our faster and faster trips to the ground. It was great fun and a real challenge till Billy's foot missed catching the spike as he slid down. Four feet before reaching the ground his scrotum was impaled on the four inch spike. Billy fell to the ground curled into a fetal position, his hands cupping his bloodied crotch. Somehow we managed to get him home. Since his parents worked, his eighty year old grandmother took control. We later learned that she sewed the ripped scrotum back in place to contain the testicles that were free hanging. A few hours at the hospital and he returned home. He was propped up on the couch when we all dropped in to see how he looked. Through a strained smile he asked, "did I win?"

The Grand Trunk Bridge

At the far end of Main Street, the train tracks dissected the town. Main Street went over the tracks on a high wooden bridge. Two supporting tunnels on either side of the tracks provided the anchors for the arching Grand Trunk Bridge. Metal plates for the cars to run on made an awful racket as the tires hummed across them. On Saturday afternoons when most of the townsfolk had gone into St. Catharines for shopping, Billie and I would stand nonchalantly atop the bridge watching the trains passing underneath. Eventually one would slow down sufficiently to allow the two wild musketeers to climb the handrail and drop the seven or eight feet into the coal car passing underneath. The northbound train eventually stopped in Thorold, at which time we clamored over the edge and down the ladder. Across the tracks we ran laughing hysterically till we reached the road back to Merritton. Two young hitch-hiking boys always managed a quick ride the eight miles home. Grandma never did figure out how we managed to get so dirty, totally covered, from head to toe.

The Volley Balls

The tunnels on either side of the tracks provided a safe haven for people who were probably doing something they weren't supposed be doing. In winter it became a windbreak from the cold and in summer a cool shelter from the sun and rain. As evidenced by the dozens of discarded bottles and cigarette and cigar butts, its secrecy was not a well kept secret. Also its close proximity to the Municipal Pool made it convenient for young boys to meet there to discuss secret plans, among other things. The Three Musketeers held many secret meetings under that bridge. After being discovered behind Grandpa's garage, experimenting with leaves rolled up in toilet paper, it was decided that any future experiments involving smoking should be confined to the bowels of the Grand Trunk Bridge.

When Davy discovered his older brother Dick's copy of Sunbathers Magazine, carefully hidden beneath his mattress, the terrible trio headed post haste for the sanctuary of the bridge. After anxiously paging through the magazine, several times, one question plagued our little minds, why did girls have to be naked to play volleyball and how do we get volleyball?

We never did get one, but something just as educational transpired one hot summer day at the municipal pool. Billie and I had met a couple of girls that we knew from school. A Deanna and Pauline. Both girls older than us. Horseplay under the water went from kidding around to a new sensation, erotic arousal. As the afternoon wore on, physical jostling and conversations took on a decidedly sexual nature. It was suggested that a more in depth discussion be continued at the bridge. It didn't take long for a few giggles and kisses to graduate to a show and tell. The excitement of seeing real girls without volleyballs was breath-taking. But nothing took my breath away like what I saw Billy and Deanna doing, half hidden in the shadows. Not wanting to appear as inexperienced as I actually was, I ventured the only question I could think of, "do you want to?" Her reply led to a moment in time more memorable than all the subsequent afternoons spent at the municipal pool. And so on that hot summer day, in the cool darkness of the Grand Trunk Bridge, I discovered that sex wasn't such a big deal, mainly because I simply had no idea what I was supposed to do, but I did learn that volleyballs played a very small part.

More summer of '46

The summer of '46 I celebrated my ninth birthday at Queenston Heights. Grandma prepared a big picnic lunch and I invited Billie Watson, his older brother Leroy, Davie Brown and his brother Dick. My Mother Dorothy and Dad Leon also came. All the guys climbed the Brock monument and later we played baseball in the wide open, very clean and green park. I quietly worried throughout the entire afternoon that when we returned to Merritton, I would once again be uprooted and have to go back with my still new Mommy and Daddy. It came as a relief when they both piled into his new car and left me, holding Grandma's hand.

Leon by now, having had ample time to pursue his quest for fame and fortune was apparently succeeding. His clothes drew quite a few comments, as did his new brown Ford sedan. Dorothy was wearing the latest fashions and flashing new jewelry. Tommy unimpressed with this nouveau riche show took every opportunity to cast barbs at Leon. Grandpa Rapsey as usual, was stoic.

But it seemed that Grandma had to be repeatedly pouring calming oil on the ever increasing troubled waters. Tommy had a succinct way of voicing his opinions of Leon. He openly enjoyed accusing Leon of being phony with an over inflated ego. How prophetic a commentary for such a young man. Perhaps Tommy simply didn't like Leon's way of denigrating him because he was "just a carpenter", and he drank "beer". Successful people drank cocktails, and wore white shirts according to the gospel of Leon Perras. Perhaps Leon felt Tommy was beneath him because of his limited education. Shades of the pot calling the kettle black. Or perhaps he just enjoyed the sense of power he believed he held over others. Tommy and Leon never did enjoy an amicable relationship.

Dorothy had recently been released from the sanitarium and they were living in a rented apartment in downtown Hamilton. Grandma told me that they were saving their money to move to a lake front home on Lake Ontario in Burlington. That meant that some day soon I would be moving again. This was not high on my wish list. I didn't like Dorothy and wasn't too sure about Leon. He frightened me.

Chapter Ten
Mommy and Daddy Again

Crying Hurts

Occasionally, I visited my "Mommy and Daddy" when they lived in Hamilton. I would spend a week-end with them. In retrospect it was probably a "breaking in" period for all of us. Dorothy, to see if she could handle the reins of motherhood. And Leon, to see if he really wanted the responsibilities and the ongoing burden of a child. I guess it was in some small way to see if I wanted to be with them, although that exact point was never raised. I was never offered a vote on the final decision. I don't recall the number of week-ends we practiced, but the end result was that I had to say goodbye to all my friends on Almond Street. Goodbye to my Grandma and Grandpa. Goodbye to the endless summers in the woods; winters filled with snowballs and forts, and goodbye to the Grand Trunk Bridge.

All of my life was packed into a single suitcase. The case and I were loaded into the back seat of the car. We drove over the Grand Trunk Bridge one last time as we headed for my new home with my semi-new parents. I couldn't stop crying. Leon's threat to give me something to really cry about did however bring an abrupt end to the tears. Tears that were soon replaced by anger. I had never felt anger for an adult before. Evidently, a true harbinger of things to come.

The first memories of living once again, with my adopted parents were at Beach Boulevard in Burlington. In the forties Burlington Beach was a long strip of land sandwiched between Hamilton Bay and its giant industries and the great and beautiful Lake Ontario. Our house sat back from the road on a predominately sand lot liberally mixed in with crab grass and sand spurs. The back of the property ended at the half buried remains of a wire fence, presumably erected many years before to prevent one from trespassing across the railway tracks to the sandy beach. Sandy is actually a poor description. Fine gravel interspersed with waterlogged remnants of past storms, washed ashore garbage from passing ships, and always the dead fish. But to a young boy, raised in the small town of Merritton, it did present many opportunities for discovery.

It was on this beach, one evening that I smoked my first punk. Punk, that piece of twig that had spent probably years floating around Lake Ontario till finally beaching itself on my small domain. My buddy next door, Bernie Butt showed me how to light the end of the stick and since the veins in the twigs had been dried out, they created fine hair like tubes for the smoke to travel. No cigarette has ever been made as strong as the smoke that filtered through the end of that branch. That experiment should have been enough to dissuade one from ever intentionally taking up the habit.

Don't Kill the Kid

Giant poplar trees bordered our yard. From somewhere high up, giant vines hung to the ground. Bernie and I spent many afternoons swinging as we envisioned Tarzan might do and even learning a flip or two. Till the day Mom saw us and complained to Dad, who promptly cut the vines off far above our heads, effectively ending our swinging. For our safety he said.

Interestingly, my safety became a major issue later that same summer. I had been playing on the beach when I developed stomach pains. Dorothy decided that I simply had too much sun and told me to sit on the porch for a while. The pain didn't subside. It became increasingly severe with each passing minute. When I couldn't stand the pain any longer I went to her in tears. She sent me to my room. As I doubled up in pain, Dorothy brought in a hot water bottle and had me hold it against my stomach.

The pain worsened. Leon arrived home from work and heard my cries. Dorothy told him of the terrible afternoon she'd had with me. Leon came in the room and in a heartbeat had diagnosed the problem. Loudly proclaiming, "Jesus Christ, Dorothy, you're going to kill the boy. He has appendicitis". They rushed me to Hamilton General Hospital for an emergency appendectomy. I heard Leon telling Grandma Rapsey, later that the appendix was so inflamed, it burst as the doctor removed it. It was not till many years later that I learned the true gravity of that episode and the inevitable end result, had Leon not come home when he did.

The warm summer on the beach slowly evolved into one of the worst winters in recent history. Living on the edge of the great lake and enduring months of frigid air blowing across giant ice floes, possibly played a large part in Leon's acceptance of an offer to move to Kitchener as Superintendent of Agencies for the London Life Insurance Company. We had lived on the beach for little more than a year.

Kitchener

Kitchener, in the early fifties, like most small towns in Canada was a virtual utopia. Though, few recognized it at the time. Businesses were thriving, street crime was practically unknown and families were raised without fear. Waterloo joined Kitchener, ultimately becoming known as the twin cities. Population at that time was about thirty-six thousand. King Street was the main street, naturally, with Queen Street being the dividing line. At this junction, the most prestigious corner in the city was the Wapler Hotel. It was the convention centerpiece frequented only by the affluent and the affluent wannabees. Lesser hotels like the Waterloo and the Mayfair catered to the more transient traveler, those with a limited budget, who didn't mind the flashing neon illuminating their room over the street. I couldn't have cared less about either.

Our first home in Kitchener was a castle. Barra Castle, at 401 Queen Street South. A three story apartment building that had turrets built across the roof-line, hence the name. It was conveniently located only six blocks from the heart of downtown Kitchener. More importantly, to me anyway, was that it was only four blocks from Victoria School. Out the back of the school was the playground, abutting Victoria Park.

The Victoria was a large open area in which to play all sorts of games. Softball, football, even fly-casting into giant canvas bull's eyes. A large lake to canoe or paddle- boat in and a quaint bridge for lovers to stand together and gaze into the future. And a very large ballpark, completely fenced in for the local softball teams. And most importantly, it was located adjacent to Joan Cook's paper route.

At twelve years old, my latest interest lay in the back room of the Tamblyn's Drug Store. There I learned the fine art of making vinegar. Big rubber gloves that went almost to my shoulders protected me from the acetic aid that I carefully measured into the clean gallon jugs. Next I filled them with water and stuck on the label. In between making vinegar and sweeping the backroom floor, I delivered prescriptions on my balloon tired C.C.M bicycle. I worked there every Saturday morning for almost a year.

Saturday afternoons I delivered The Liberty Magazine. It was during this endeavor that I learned an important marketing tool. It was called "T" prospecting. Each time I delivered the magazine to a customer, I also asked the neighbors on each side and across the street if they would like a subscription. It worked well and I soon built my route to over fifty customers. I made the royal sum of two dollars and fifty cents a week, plus tips. I had to save two dollars and could spend, wisely of course the remaining fifty cents. I so wished there was a way to increase my earnings. Someone once said, be careful what you wish for.

Monetary Opportunities

One beautiful, sunny afternoon on my way home from school, my wish was about to be granted, in a way I never even dreamed of. In my class was a girl named Joan Cook. She had a paper route in my neighborhood. One afternoon, as I walked home alongside her, making small talk, I reached my street where I started to turn off. She asked me quite out of the blue, if I would accompany her for the rest of her route. When I declined, informing her of my pending important plans, she suggested that I might earn twenty-five cents simply for accompanying her. And I didn't need to carry her paper bag either. Needless to say, I accompanied her two or three times a week.

An added benefit of walking with her was that the route ended in the woods behind Victoria Park. Joan and I shared many special moments that summer, talking and learning about each other in the privacy of those woods. Equally important, was the adding of additional coin to my purse. Coin that did not have to be reported to Mom or Dad.

The Gorillas

As a tall, skinny, twelve year old boy wearing glasses, I seem to be the opponent of choice for any bully wanting to show off his pugilistic skills. I would never qualify as a nerd. My grades were mediocre at best. Neither athletic nor most popular, I plodded my way through school day by day. However hard I tried to distance myself from these gorillas, they inevitably would find me and use me to further their reputations as a force to be reckoned with.

One day, in the middle of the asphalt basketball court, I found myself once again in a familiar predicament. After unceremoniously being tripped and tossed to the ground again and again, I closed my eyes, climbed to my feet and desperately charged headlong into his unprotected stomach. As he doubled over, I threw my arms around his neck and brought him headfirst into the pavement. Blind rage and rampant fear caused me to slam his head again and again into the court asphalt. Suddenly, the strong hands of the Principal lifted me up and off the now prostrate boy.

It was most fortunate for me that the principal had chosen the right moment to look out from his office window in time to see me being slammed to the ground. It did exonerate me somewhat. However, because of the boy's bloodied head it was necessary to report the entire incident to Leon and Dorothy. Though this did not sit well with them, it did elevate me in the eyes of my classmates when I returned to school. Suddenly, I had friends. I was in. Perhaps there was a lesson to be learned from this. I don't know, but I was finally part of "the Gang".

The Cap-Gun Heist

Under the heading, boys will be boys, our gang, about eight of us, used to make, on occasion, forays into Woolworth Five & Dime. We were sort of like a mini Ocean's Eleven. We even had a "look-out" and a "diverter" and a specific brand of cap gun we planned to pilfer. After weeks of our unlawful activities, most of the gang would come to school well armed. Two or three cap guns under our jerseys and pockets full of caps. Our downfall started when the newest junior member of the gang failed to obey our number one creed. "No-one goes alone". He did, and he got caught.

That would have been acceptable to us because he was young and inexperienced, but it became very unacceptable, when he blew the whistle on every one of us. We all learned of this on our way to school the next morning. The groundskeeper for the ballpark must have been scratching his head when he came upon a couple dozen brand new cap guns, all hastily thrown over the park fence, by boys trying to rid themselves of incriminating evidence. Needless to say this incident added a fresh batch of hi-test fuel to an already volatile situation at home.

Especially when one of Kitchener's finest showed up at the Perras door, looking for Bobbie. Mom and Dad were furious, angry, upset and most of all, concerned; concerned with what the neighbors might think.

This incident further validated Leon and Dorothy's fear that they had been cursed with a real life version of the "bad seed". Little did they know just how well that "seed" would flourish under their regime.

Best Friend

My best friend Eddie Pihowich and I walked to school together most every day. Our route took us along the ballpark fence. A quite non-descript unpainted fence. However, right in the middle of the fence was a ticket booth. About seven feet wide with two windows cut out and vertical bars to facilitate the sale of tickets on game days. The aged boards, warped and separated, made it quite easy to peer inside. The booth was devoid of anything except two wooden stools for the ticket sellers to sit on. But most interestingly, the door that leads into this empty shack had a padlock on it. Presumably to keep the curious out. Had there never been a lock, we probably would have just kept walking. But, the lock was a challenge.

Across the street a lady had planted grass seed and erected a rope fence around the perimeter of her yard. The rope was supported by several pieces of steel pipe. The perfect tool for prying the lock off the empty ticket booth. Unfortunately, prying it off proved to be considerably more difficult than we anticipated and consequently took a long time and a great deal of hammering for us to complete the task. Sadly, for us, there was just enough time for the lady across the street to call the police.

The ride home in the police car, the blue coat escort up the stairs to the apartment and the call to Leon's office proved too much for Mom and Dad. In one short three week period, I had had a series of misadventures, that ended up with myself and a psychiatrist together in my bedroom, trying to establish if I was truly the boy from hell or just a young lad on his way to becoming a career criminal.

Leon told the psychiatrist that he intended to sit in on the interview. The psychiatrists sternly forbid his presence. One of the few times in my life when I saw Leon forced to do someone else's bidding. He wasn't happy. He was even less happy when the doctor came out of the room with me in tow, sat all three of us on the couch, like school children and advised them that Bobbie was no better or no worse than any other young man his age.

I found it interesting, even at my tender age, to find this doctor questioning me about my relationship with Leon. Did we go to football games, hockey games? Did we do father and son things. Hunting, fishing, playing ball. I explained to him, as best I could, that Leon had to work days and nights in order to provide the good lifestyle that we currently enjoy. Oh yes, I already knew all the words to that song. Consequently, he didn't have time to play games with me. At twelve years old, I told myself that it really didn't matter to me. But it did bother me though, and as I grew older, I noticed more and more frequently, that all the other guys went places and did things with their Dads. Their Dads all seemed to have time to participate in their kid's lives. I guess they weren't as privileged as I was, living this enviable lifestyle.

Strangely, he did seem to have time for hockey games, football games, golf games and curling and hunting and fishing trips, with all his friends. I guess I never ever qualified for membership to that elite group. Someday I vowed, I would be good enough to be accepted.

The Collegiate Boys

The biggest non-industrial building in town was the high school. Originally called K.C.I., Kitchener Collegiate Institute. I never attended K.C.I. By the time I arrived, it had been changed to the almost impossible to write-on-one-line, "The Kitchener-Waterloo Collegiate and Vocational Institute". This institute of higher learning offered a freedom I had never experienced in Public school. It was here that I learned about cigarettes, sloe gin and eight ball. I also discovered music, art and writing. None of the aforementioned added anything to my future earning capacities.

I started high school with the usual array of early teenage misapprehensions. I was just beginning to get used to being the top dog in the eighth grade. Sort of the big fish syndrome. But now starting over, as it were, in the ninth grade, was much akin to my first day at kindergarten. Except in this school everyone was superior to me. Playground time was replaced with gym class. Games were replaced by exercises. Books with colorful pictures were replaced by tomes of incomprehensible hieroglyphics.

Teachers who had once seemed more of a friend than a teacher were now granite icons of higher learning. In the public schools, older students were looked up to and almost revered. As ninth graders, we were the bottom feeders. This did not promise to be a fun trip.

Chapter Eleven
High School

What Price Education?

Bob - Gail Preston - Blackie

Her name was Gail Preston. She lived in a quiet suburb in Waterloo in a two story yellow brick house. It had a small porch overlooking a postage-sized front lawn. The porch provided room to sit on the rails but not enough for a chair.

Gail was fourteen, dark brown hair, almost black eyes and a dazzling white smile. She could charm the birds out of the trees. She was my first real true love. Mrs. Preston would have been my second love, were she not Gail's mother. She would bring snacks out to the porch for us to munch on. She'd listen to all the stories Gail and I told about our school activities. Mr. Preston would stop and sit with us a while, after work, before he went in the house. They were interested in their daughter and their daughter's friends.

I lived in Westmount, sort of a nob hill, about eight blocks away. I made the first of many mistakes telling Dorothy about my new found love. This led to one of her many tirades about my being too young to be in love. Too young to be interested in girls. Too inexperienced to know my own mind. School studies were priority. Social life is not important. When she ran out of personal reasons for my not pursuing a social life with Gail, she began the economic argument. My father worked too hard for his son to associate with those people who lived on the other side of the tracks. Her father was blue collar. We were white collar! Her neighborhood was middle class; ours was upper class! Ultimately, I was forbidden to see her.

In my first year of high school, I made several friends. There was "Spike", and "Whitey" and "Slip" and "Blackie" and yesterday's equivalent of today's nerd, "Junebug".

Top Row Paul-Red-Spike-Max
Front row Blackie -Whitey - Hugo

The Freshmen
**Back Row: Paul, Red, Spike, Max, Front Row:
Blackie, Whitey, Bob, and Heinrich**

Junebug's real name was Johnny Shiel. He was an "A" student, in everything except gym and girls. He coached me in the sciences and I helped him with girls. His mother was so perfect in every way. She could have replaced June Cleaver, the "Beaver's" mom. For every flaw that my Dorothy saw and amplified in me, she saw positive things. Junebug's home became my second home. Many nights as I closed my eyes to sleep I prayed that I could have a Mrs. Shiel for a mother. I'd had so many different ones before, why couldn't I have just one more? She was friends with Mrs. Preston and neither of them could understand why my mother was so adamant about my not associating with Gail. In spite of Dorothy's threats, I still saw and even dated Gail. A lot of our times together were as a result of our information network we set up. I would go over to Junebug's house, he was on the A-list, and from there I'd high tail it up the street to Gail's. When it was suppertime Dorothy would phone Mrs. Shiel to send me home. A quick phone call to Mrs. Preston would give me ample time to head for home. Dorothy was none the wiser. It was a good arrangement for all concerned. Gail and I eventually outgrew our puppy love and she and I and her family remained friends for many years. As did Junebug and me.

I was tall and I was slim, but I was never a good student. Not actually a bad student either. Actually a mediocre one would be a more apt description. I invoked Leon's wrath on a quarterly basis when each report card showed a failing grade in French. Leon Perras, a true Frenchman, with a son who couldn't pass French! Sad but true. I could read it and I could generally speak it. I just couldn't write it. And a passing grade was dependant on your ability to write it. His eyes would immediately search out the French grade and the tirade would begin. All other grades would be ignored. They didn't matter.

I once volunteered the unacknowledged fact that Leon himself never learned to master writing French, because of his limited primary schooling. That presented argument did nothing to endear myself to him. I learned to shut up, and survive. No one argues with Leon and wins. At least not in his house. A fact that I had, all too painfully proven true.

Girls Music & Girls

In high school, everyone gets into varying degrees of trouble. I was no different. About average, I'd say. Friday night sock-hops always presented many and varied means to achieve some degree of notoriety.

Although I never studied music, I was born with a natural ability for the keyboard. If I could hear it, I could eventually play it. A few of my friends also enjoyed similar talents. During Friday night dances, after enjoying the company of some young ladies on the dance floor, we would eventually leave the gymnasium and sneak through the bushes to the corner of the building that housed the music room. A penknife blade unlatched the high towering window and we were soon wailing out rock and roll and jazz and even a few romantic ones. The latter because of the admiring girls outside the windows, faces and lips pressed to the glass.

It was my first taste of true attention from the opposite sex. For several weeks we had a ball every Friday night in the music room. But it was our popularity that led to our undoing. The hand full of fans eventually grew to a quite noticeable crowd. So much so that the dance chaperons began to wonder why a large portion of the Friday night crowd was vanishing. Their subsequent investigation led to our discovery. Ergo, a budding career in music was tragically cut short. But the euphoria from the applause and the sweet taste remained with me forever.

The downside was that we all were punished with 45 minute detentions after school for three months. The school's punishment was nothing compared to the sentence I received from Leon and Dorothy. I remember mostly his anger when Leon ranted about the how I besmirched his fine name. I didn't dare ask what besmirched meant. Dorothy about this time discovered a new use for her large wooden mixing spoons. Apparently, my Grandpa Perras had long ago disposed of his leather-stropping belt so she was forced to be creative.

A large wooden spoon is quite a formidable weapon in the hands of a determined woman. Six on the left and six on the right bring up sizable red welts. Fortunately, they soon dissipate and are not visible to outsiders. Whoever said it, was certainly right, love does indeed hurt. I was punished so I wouldn't forget. I guess it worked. I never forgot.

Jeremy Hughes

One of my closest friends that lived in our socially acceptable neighborhood was the son of a prominent dentist.

Jerry Hughes was three years older than I and could frequently regale me with stories of his dates, his hunting trips with his dad and also share with me exciting times during his summer as a junior forest ranger. It was with Jerry that I learned to drive at about age fifteen. After several side trips into shrubs and a couple of curbs, I eventually mastered it well enough to apply and receive my license on my sixteenth birthday. However, Dr. Hugh's car unfortunately, probably needed a few extra alignments during my learning period. Driving up over curbs does have a tendency to throw out the alignment. We never felt it propitious to advise him of my lessons.

Jerry also took me hunting with him. We both had twenty-two bore rifles, which were perfect for ridding farmers of their number one pests, the groundhog. Those same rifles became a catalyst for an event that almost ended our young lives.

One Christmas, Jerry received a new rifle as a present. His next door neighbor, a pretty young girl of sixteen was visiting her Aunt and Uncle for the holidays. Jerry asked his Dad if he could take the girl and me out to the country to demonstrate his prowess with a rifle. His Dad agreed and we were off in Dr. Hughes brand new Ford sedan.

Everything was fine till we entered a curve at high speed on a gravel road. At seventy miles an hour the car rocketed off the road, became airborne and tumbled end over end ripping off the doors and hood, finally coming to a stop upside down in a farmer's newly ploughed field.

Jerry was pinned under the car and the girl had been thrown out on one of the first flips. I was under the dash upside down. I unwound myself and crawled out, racing around the car to Jerry's side. His lower body was pinned by the roof frame. Jerry evidently not in great pain but frightened half to death screamed for me to get him out from under the car. I bent down, straddled and grabbed the exposed frame and lifted the car; two inches, five inches, eight inches. Jerry clawing at the muddied field slowly extricated himself, stood up and checked to see if there was anything broken. "I'm okay" he said, "how about you?" Shaking like I leaf," I said, "but still in one piece".

About then we noticed a figure covered in mud from head to toe, running down the hill. Tears left white trails across her cheeks as she hugged us. "I thought we were goners" she said between sobs. She had been thrown out on one of the first flips and evidently ended up pancaked into the soft newly harrowed field.

The next day the local newspaper, the Kitchener Record featured a picture of the demolished car with the headline, *"Miracle Car- Three teenagers walk away!"*

Mr. and Mrs. Hughes were so relieved that everyone was all right, they both cried tears of joy. However, it appeared that Leon and Dorothy's main concern was that I didn't seek permission from them to go for the drive, and furthermore, the Hughes family just might feel that Leon should pay a share of the damages. Consequently he never even attempted to contact Mr. Hughes.

Later when Jerry and I discussed it, he said his Dad only said, "That's what insurance is for". I remembered thinking that he seemed to have a better understanding of the reason for insurance than Leon, who actually made his living selling it. Three years later the damage I inflicted to the lumbar region of my spine by lifting the car, kept me out of the Canadian Army. Quite possibly a good thing.

Chapter Twelve
Leon's Bar

Appearances

Doctor and Mrs. Hughes were not fans of Leon and Dorothy Perras. They knew of them but they never associated with them socially. They did however become acutely familiar with their corporal punishment techniques through an incident, which unfortunately, ended with me on their doorstep.

The basement of our John Boulevard home was originally unfinished, as were most at that time. Leon and Dorothy, after a dinner party at one of the neighbors, who happened to be a financially well off lawyer, returned home excitedly talking about his finished family room. He had tiled the floor for dancing, and had even built a small bar so two or three of his buddies could "sidle up to the bar", as it were.

Leon had to have a "Rec" room too. Our basement's main feature was a furnace room and Grandma Rapsey's player piano against the wall. Which incidentally, I had become rather adept at, by now. My week-end, and after school time became "painting time". Gallons and gallons of base primer were spread, followed by a pastel yellow. Apparently, to give the illusion of a happy room. Then the real work began. A carpenter by the name of Thomas laid out two by fours on the floor for the beginning of Leon's bar. Only not just big enough for two or three guys, it was a full twelve feet long. Bigger and better, that was Leon's motto.

The rail was padded red leather with polished brass buttons. Quite attractive, if you like garish. The surface of the bar was to be Leon's showpiece. It was inlaid maple strips. It was beautiful, but it was rough. Someone had to sand it. This was before electric sanders. I cannot recall the number of afternoons and evenings I spent sanding that tribute to Leon's ego. Time I would dearly have preferred playing baseball or some other teenage activity.

But I do recall vividly the day he came home and called me to help him unload the trunk of his car. Laid out in all its past glory was a large, very heavy ornate half-door of some kind. Leon proudly explained that he bought it from the bank. They were redecorating and didn't feel that the swinging door would fit in with their new upscale look. Leon had the carpenter attach it across the end of the bar. The door weighed a ton and looked totally out of place, as Dorothy plaintively suggested. It didn't matter. He had a bigger bar than the neighbors and a door that no one else had. Leon was happy.

Hide the Shirt

High school was generally a good time for me. Actually, anywhere away from Leon and Dorothy was good for me.

At school, all the guys wore jeans and white T-shirts. Except me. I wore a pressed dress shirt. My jeans had a crease. My shoes had a shine. If I wasn't nerd, or a geek, I sure looked the part. So, I scuffed my shoes and folded my shirt and left it beneath a bush down the street from the school. I rolled my T-shirt sleeves and when off the school grounds, I carried my cigarettes in my sleeve. I fitted in.

On the way home, I rescued my fresh shirt from under the shrub, wiped the dirt from my shoes and ate several handfuls of grass, hoping the chlorophyll would cover the telltale smoker's breath. Actually the grass did little other than give me green teeth. But since we only smoked during lunch hour, by the time I headed home, most of the tell tale aroma had dissipated. Besides, I never really enjoyed smoking, it was just necessary to be a part of the in crowd.

Chapter Thirteen
The Tug of War

Everything Leads Out the Door

It's hard to determine, even after so many years, exactly what was the catalyst for the discontent in our family. Leon's totalitarian approach to family life; or Dorothy's propensity for lying when ever she might become the target for Leon's wrath; or was it the continuing conflict created daily by an impressionable young man? Doubtless it was a combination of all factors, but a most predominant factor was the constant interference by Gwen and James.

I was about twelve when it started. A game for Jim and Gwen. A tug of war between the Perras family and the Burnett family. Young Bobbie was the pawn that each side wanted to win. The psychological impact on this impressionable boy was never for a minute considered.

I was fourteen when Leon and Dorothy agreed to deliver me to Gwen for a two week vacation. She and Jim lived in Guelph, only fifteen miles away. That summer they had a confectionery booth in the middle of a beautiful park in downtown Guelph. They sold sodas, chocolate bars, gum and other assorted confections. To this day I recall the aroma every time I pick up a package of Wrigley's. It was a wonderful two weeks. I had total access to any snacks I wanted and of course I was at the heart of Gwen's attentions.

Gwen and Jim never had any of the problems associated with raising a young boy. Grandma Rapsey handled that burden. And now they had the opportunity to enjoy the bragging rights with none of the costs.

Dorothy and Leon were quite amenable to my visits with Gwen. Since it afforded them their much desired private time. After all, they had been apart for six years while Dorothy recuperated in the hospital. But along with the benefits for Leon, a pattern was developing. Each visit I found Gwen being more and more lenient. Understanding I called it. Each visit we spent far too much time talking about Leon and Dorothy. I learned first hand the burning hatred that Jimmy Burnett harbored for Leon even after so many years. Their criticisms never ended.

There's little doubt that many of my attitudes were formed during those summers spent with them. Besides being their 'special boy', I was also allowed to smoke, drink beer and look at Jim's girly magazines. What teenager wouldn't die for a set of such parents? And then it all would end upon returning to the Perras household.

The Good Times?

I had developed quite a skill in archery. Along with a couple of friends we would trek through the trees and bushes in search of big game that we could bag. Most times we would succeed only in losing or breaking arrows. Since I made the arrows myself, the arrows themselves weren't the main loss. But the steel broad heads and tri-heads costs about a dollar apiece. I needed to either shoot straighter or increase my archery budget. Fortunately I found a way to do both.

There were only three skills that I possessed that Leon was proud of. One was my shoe shining abilities. I shined his golf shoes, his work shoes and his formal black shoes, every week. His requirements were that he could see his reflected image. Spit polish became my silent mantra. Seldom did they ever pass his military-like inspections upon first presentation.

The second talent was my ability to play the piano by ear. As a special treat for his party attendees, I was called upon to provide background music. And if the party revved up early enough, and I hadn't yet reached my bed time, I stepped up the pace to provide dance music. I believe he was truly proud and envious of this innate ability.

The third talent was most special to me. Leon, when he had the "boys" over, would call for me to bring out my bow and arrows. The back yard was two tiered going out about seventy-five yards. Leon would with great flourish stab an arrow in the ground. Pace down fifty paces. And with a wave of his arm cry out to no one in particular, "every hit gets you three". That was our agreement. Every arrow I hit and shattered from fifty yards, he would buy me three new ones. A half hour of performing would inevitably net me a dozen new arrows.

Unfortunately not everyone was enamored with my archery skills.

One Saturday afternoon I was in our front yard watching crows fly into the giant oak tree across the road from our house. I had on several occasions stood twenty or thirty yards out from the tree in the middle of the field, and when the crows took off from the tree branches, for the adjacent woods, I would shoot over my head at them, eventually scoring a hit or two.

No one complained, because crows were bad. But, this particular Saturday, I spied a squirrel running from the roadside to the big oak. Halfway up the trunk he stopped and looked around. It was about forty yards from where I stood. I targeted the squirrel and let the shaft fly. To my amazement and delight I scored a bull's eye.

To my everlasting dismay, Dorothy had been looking out the front window throughout the whole episode. Her shrieking could have been heard a block away. My punishment of grounding for two weeks was nothing compared to the confiscation of my bow and arrows. I don't believe I ever took them back up. Lesson learned: crows bad; squirrels good, and always look over your shoulder for Dorothy.

Deny, Deny, Deny

Their fights and arguments seemed to grow more frequent with each passing year. They fought over money, over his drinking, which was actually only social drinking, but he did tend to become rather loud and boastful after a few rum and cokes; And most vigorously, over his working way past the acceptable hour for selling insurance.

I may have been a young teenager, but I wasn't stupid. I knew what the fights were about. Most of the bigger fights would end with Leon screaming for her to pack her god damn bags and go back to the other side of the tracks where she belonged. This from an eighth grade drop out.

I would go to sleep at night trying to decide which one I would go live with when they divorced. Dorothy would promise that when they divorced she would take me with her, so he couldn't get his hands on me. Leon had his moments too. He vowed that I would never have to go and live with that bitch. Though I waited and prayed, it never happened.

The end result was that for the next week, she served silent suppers and he worked late, late hours. Personally, I kind of enjoyed it. It was one of the few periods when I was basically ignored.

Dorothy lived in constant fear of Leon's wrath as did I. If she said or did something that upset him or something that he disapproved of, she developed her own answer to redirect his wrath. Dorothy, would simply deny, deny, deny. The end result was that I became the recipient of his anger. Denying didn't work for me. I was never afforded that privilege.

At sixteen, the biggest event of the year was the high school prom. Every girl lived for it and every guy outwardly hated it but secretly couldn't wait for it. I was no different.

On the Friday night sock-hops when I wasn't jamming in the music room, I would lean against the gym wall with the other guys, carefully picking out the girl who we felt was least likely to turn down an offer to dance.

I spied a petite blonde, in a big crinoline, dancing with her girlfriend. I knew her girlfriend, Marion Schlachter. A brunette who knew her way around the dance floor and always drew a lot of attention. The blonde smiled at me. I asked and she accepted.

We danced. I was smitten. Her name was Angela.

Angela Marie Diebolt. 1953

She lived across town. For the next several months I contributed heavily to the cross town bus profits. As the prom date drew closer, I talked frequently with Dorothy about what I'd wear and what type of corsage to buy for Angela. We always ended our discussion with my plea for an extended "be-home-by" time. Eleven o'clock was the bewitching hour. It meant catching a bus home by ten-thirty. That meant I'd be saying goodnight to Angela at the gym door.

The day of the prom finally arrived and I was quite giddy with anticipation. Four o'clock and I was already showered. My clothes were laid out across my bed and my last decision was, which tie is best. I picked up two and went to the kitchen to get Dorothy's opinion. Big mistake!

Buckle Imprints Last Forever

Leon was enthroned in his overstuffed red leather chair, reading, Dorothy was preparing for supper. I came out of the bedroom carrying the two ties. In the kitchen I showed them to Dorothy and asked her choice. Before she could respond, Leon shouted, ties for what? I walked to his chair and held up the ties and told him that I couldn't decide which tie to wear to the prom tonight. His reply floored me! "Prom", he roared, "what prom, nobody asked me about any prom". My first reaction was to laugh. I thought he was joking with me. He wasn't. "Dar-thy" he bellowed. We both knew what Dar-thy instead of Dorothy meant. "Get in here!" She meekly scurried through the dining room to stand penitently at his feet. "What's this about a prom" he interrogated? Dorothy immediately shrank into her deny mode. "I don't know a thing about it. This is the first I've heard of it." I stared at her incredulously. "Mom, are you serious? We've been talking and planning for tonight for a month".

Her reply left me in shock. She looked at Leon and told him with a straight face, that this was just a ploy so I can get out of the house. I turned to her and screamed, "You're a liar, a god damn liar". I turned to Leon in time to see him fly out of his chair. Papers and books went flying everywhere. Dorothy jumped back trying to determine who he was headed for. He grabbed me by the shirt collar with both hands and screamed "you will not talk like that to your Mother". I screamed back, "what the hell do you call someone who is lying through their teeth?"

A flat hand across the back of my head sent me spinning down the hall towards my bedroom. I got to my feet in time to catch another swing. In the bedroom he screamed for Dorothy to come in. She scurried down the hall as he flung me over the bed. "I think it's time we taught this boy some manners" he said as he pulled his belt through the loops. "Dorothy, pull his pants down" he commanded as he crossed my hands above my head and knelt on them. Dorothy pulled my pants and underwear to my ankles. He handed her the leather belt. She commenced to whip me across my bare buttocks. She managed four or five lashes before Leon noticed that she was holding the long end of the belt and the buckle was slicing open flesh with each swing.

He told her to turn the belt around. I can't remember how many more lashes I got. But I remember the tears. Tears of pain, of anger and of embarrassment. At sixteen I would eventually get past the pain and perhaps even the anger. But to be stripped naked from the waist down and whipped like a wayward runaway slave was the ultimate in degradation.

Even today, these many, many years later, I lack words to describe the total humiliation and debasement suffered at their hands. I still carry the physical scars of the buckle as a reminder.

Later Leon instructed Dorothy to call Angela and confirm if there was in fact a prom. Upon confirmation he permitted my attendance with the stipulation that any additional punishment would be determined the next morning. Punishment for what? I had done nothing wrong. What would any future punishment be for? Because of Dorothy's innate fear of Leon's wrath, she once again spewed her venomous lies which this time resulted in a permanent reminder carved into my side.

Chapter Fourteen
My Safe House

The Magic Condom

One of the pastimes for the in crowd at high school was to pool our money and get a senior to buy a package of condoms. Six of us each got one. Some guys would blow theirs up and parade them in front of the giggling girls; others would fill them with water and try to drop them out the second story window on unsuspecting students below. Others, like me kept it in the back of the wallet, just in case. Mine was there for so long it had dried out and was on the verge of disintegrating. But at sixteen it was still an acceptable status symbol. But its ultimate cost was far more than I ever could have anticipated.

It was Saturday morning. I was in the furnace room cleaning and polishing Leon's golf shoes, preparatory to his game Sunday. Leon was taking stock of his liquor supply, behind the bar. I heard Dorothy come down the stairs. I tried to make out what Dorothy was so upset about, when the furnace room door burst open. Leon charged into room, collared me by the back of my neck and dragged me up to the bar.

Sitting on the bar was my tired, dried and dirty condom package. "What the hell is that" he thundered! "Where did you get it, I lamely countered." "I ask the questions here. You answer. Now explain this". I tried to explain by telling him that all the guys had them. I tried to point out that it was so old it was useless. Then I made the mistake of demanding to know how Dorothy came to be in possession of something that was buried in my wallet and deep in my jeans pocket. She in a near frenzy screamed that it fell out of my jeans when she was cleaning. I told her rather emphatically that she was a damn liar. Wham! Boy, sometimes I never learn.

I never saw it coming. Leon nailed me with a roundhouse that threw me against the wall. By now, Leon's screaming about me being a whore just like Gwen, and a few other expletives, I've forgotten. I scrambled to my feet in time to be knocked down again. I can't say I remember any rationale for what happened next, but I knew I wasn't going to just lie there and have the crap beat out of me. I lunged at him from a crouch. He bounced off the bar to the floor. I landed on top, but he outweighed me by sixty pounds and quickly flipped me off and started throwing punches, anywhere and everywhere.

I'd had enough; I scrambled halfway up the stairs before he caught me. He pulled me backwards down the stairs and the momentum carried both of us into his precious swinging door. It ripped off the hinges, splintering the bar and landing on top of me. Leon was in an uncontrolled rage.

Stomping on top of the door, trying to connect with my head he kept hollering "look at my bar, look at what you've done. Get out you bastard, get out, get out!"

I didn't need another invitation. I raced up the stairs and ran outside, tears streaming down my cheeks. I ran blindly, as the blood ran into my eyes and down the side of my face.

Mrs. Hughes almost had a heart attack when I burst into her kitchen. I apologized because I had no one else to turn to. The Hughes's house had become my "safe house" where I was always welcome.

Mrs. Hughes patched up the cuts, salved the bruises and quieted me down. Fortunately this was to be the last of many emergency trips I had made to her sanctuary over the past four years.

She called Dorothy and advised her that I would be staying with them for a few days, until everyone calmed down. Dorothy objected and threatened to call the police. Mrs. Hughes told her that she thought that would be an excellent idea. Evidently Dorothy decided against bringing in the police. Unfortunately, Leon simply wasn't the type to calm down and Dorothy always followed Leon's lead, and I certainly would never calm down enough to forgive and forget. That final scarring was the beginning of the end.

Jim & Gwen vs. Leon & Dorothy

The next day after a long discussion with Mrs. Hughes, and Jeremy, we all agreed that it was time for a major change. It was obvious that my home life was not going to change, so perhaps a complete life style change was in order.

I called Gwen in Guelph and Mrs. Hughes spoke with her. She explained as best she could as to the seriousness of the latest altercations with Leon and the unwillingness of Dorothy to prevent them. And in fact her actual participation. Mrs. Hughes suggestion that I visit with them for a while was met with complete agreement.

Two hours later Jim and Gwen knocked on the Hughes front door. Jim was eager for a confrontation with Leon. It was decided against any meeting at this time. Jeremy and I talked in his room while the four adults discussed the best recourse. The end result was that we left within the hour for Guelph. Surprisingly, Leon and Dorothy didn't bother to start looking for me until the next day.

A phone call to the Hughes disclosed my whereabouts. The next day an angry Leon alternately berated, censured, cursed and threatened, Jim and then Gwen over the phone. For three days the Burnetts talked with their lawyers as to what they could legally do. At the same time Leon was in meetings with his legal council.

Gwen and Jim wanted to keep me away from Leon and Dorothy, if only to keep me safe from any more physical outbursts. Leon and Dorothy wanted my return because, well because, it was what Leon wanted. Besides how would they explain my sudden disappearance?

For five days I lived in Guelph. I reveled in my new found freedom. In retrospect, I see more clearly how I was merely the pawn in a power struggle between two couples that had been simmering for over a decade. Starting with Leon's belittling his baby brother Ralph's choice of girlfriend. The only one who evidently spurned any of Leon's advances.

Leon always hated to lose. And this fight with the Burnettes was no different. The prize or trophy was inconsequential. He would win, at any cost. And he did. A call from the RCMP advising the Burnetts that unless they returned an underage boy to his adopted parents, they would be issuing a warrant. For kidnapping! An ensuing call to the attorney resulted in a long quiet drive from Guelph to Kitchener.

The Meeting

As the three of us entered the front door, Leon motioned for Jim and Gwen to go to the living room; I was pointed to my bedroom. Gwen spun around between Leon and me and defiantly told him that this was about Bobbie and by god Bobbie was going to be in the room during the discussions. Leon said nothing and slid into his red leather chair. Dorothy sat in her Queen Anne upright and Jim and Gwen shared the couch. I sat on the cushion in the bay window, discretely out of the sight line. Leon commenced the discussion by outlining the points of law in his favor as laid out by his attorney. Jim cut him off in mid sentence, by advising him that if there was any possibility of their legally keeping me, they wouldn't be there at all. Jim stood up walked over to Leon, looked down on him, pointed his finger at him and said, "you've beat this kid for the last time". If I ever hear that you laid a hand on him again, I won't be going to my lawyer's, I'll be coming for you". There was no further discussion.

As they arose to leave, I handed Gwen a silver cigarette case she had given me. I told her I wouldn't be needing it any more. Gwen looked at both of them and said, "I gave it to him. It is his." She looked at Dorothy and said, "it is not yours." Then she looked at Leon who was still sitting and said it was not his either. "Do not take it away from him."

Then without a word, they walked out, leaving Leon and Dorothy still sitting. I walked to the door with them. Gwen hugged me and said "don't ever be afraid of him again". And they left.

The silver cigarette case lay on the kitchen counter for several days. Dorothy only once referred to it. She said she would not give it to me. If I wanted it, I would have to walk over and pick it up. I never did. I knew better. I still had to live in this house. It disappeared from the counter top a week later. Any smoking from that time on became a totally covert operation. Surprisingly, I never did acquire a taste for it. Smoking made me woozy, brought tears to my eyes and it made me cough. But I did it anyway, out of rebelliousness. It added yet another brick in the wall between us.

Chapter Fifteen
Free at Last

Bad decisions can last a lifetime.

A sage once mused, hindsight may make you a philosopher, but foresight will make you a millionaire. Had I not made the next decision, my life's direction from age sixteen would have probably have been diametrically opposite from the course I chose. I may have become a millionaire, instead of writing this book.

Though Leon felt he was guiding my life with his iron hand, I felt a great sense of being totally lost and alone. Nothing was gained from the Jim and Gwen fiasco. Nothing was changed. The issues that precipitated the beatings were only the tip of the iceberg. To me, the beating was purely physical, I would recover from it. The belting scars would heal. But what was never addressed was individuality. I was a teenager and had always been forbidden to close my bedroom door. I dressed in the far corner away from the hall, so Dorothy might not casually drop in on the pretense of checking on something. I was deprived a basic fundamental right, privacy.

The Bathroom

I was a teenager and Dorothy was still walking into the bathroom while I was in the bath-tub, where she would do a visual inspection of my privates to confirm that I had properly washed the area. She checked the toilet after I used it, to see if I over sprayed. And a found droplet meant I had to wash the whole toilet. I began sitting down to pee so she wouldn't be able to find any drops. I often wondered how many of Leon's sprays I took the blame for.

I remember the shame and fear I felt when awakening from sleep to see a tent pole lifting the covers and Dorothy cautioning me I'd best not be making any mess on her sheets. Reminding me frequently about "dirty" thoughts in my sleep resulting in stains. These dirty thoughts were bad, bad sins.

My closet was always left wide open; on the pretext of her checking that my clothes were hung straight. I knew it was to check my jackets and pants pockets for any kind of contraband that she could expose. The bathroom door was never, never to be locked when I was using it. The premise was that there was nothing that I needed to do in the bathroom that needed privacy.

Their privacy was a totally different thing. The bathroom door was always closed and locked. Their bedroom door was always closed. Even during the day. I was not permitted to set one foot in there. The only exception to the rule was when I would wake Leon from his four o'clock nap, for supper. I leaned inside and gently called to him, thereby awaking him without the need to touch him or even enter the sanctuary.

Sanding Expertise

Around the house I did all the usual things a teenage boy was expected to do. I took out the garbage, cut the lawn, cleaned the garage, shoveled snow, and washed windows. Inside I was taught and became quite proficient at ironing, laundry, vacuuming, washing and waxing floors. By sixteen I had become a creditable cook. All of the above became invaluable talents later in life. As a single man, for many years, I certainly appreciated the skills I had been taught. But appreciation for one special talent I had apparently perfected never left our living room.

Dorothy being a dark brunette had a luxurious growth of hair on her head and her legs. This was in the pre-Nair era. Leg razors that were the choice of the day had a tendency to nick and cut. Dorothy however preferred sand paper pads; fine grit pads that one would rub up and down the calves and anywhere else there was hair. She would lie on the couch and scrunch her dress up against her private area and I would sit on the floor in front of her. I was told many times that I was doing a really, really good job. Of all the many household chores that I felt I excelled at, this was the one chore Dorothy said was our private secret. Leon always said I did a great job for him, sanding the bar downstairs. He just never knew that Dorothy too availed herself of my sanding abilities. I felt that this covert chore might someday serve to save me from Dorothy's ire, so I performed it with a quiet satisfaction.

After being uprooted more times than I can remember, it appeared that it was fast approaching that time again. Leon, Dorothy and I had reached an impasse. After the big blowup, Leon and I ceased all conversations. Dorothy was moody and taciturn. Tension was a constant.

Then one day something happened that changed the whole atmosphere in the house. They sat me down and informed me that I was about to have a baby sister. I looked up and down Dorothy. Nope she wasn't the one. Evidently, they had been in negotiations with adoption agencies for quite some time. They had finally been notified that they were approved. A baby girl was being delivered the next day. I was shocked that they were approved. I was also surprised that as a sixteen year old, no one felt the need to interview me for my opinions. However I was concerned for her future but certainly would never express those feelings out loud. But I need not have worried. That three month old bundle exploded on the scene! Rainbows flowed across the sky, sunshine washed away the gray; and love permeated Leon's house. As Leon's greatest love affair was starting, my departure plans were already being formulated. I had made my decision.

Chapter Sixteen
All Babies are Beautiful

Deborah Leone

Debbie was a beautiful baby. Dark curly hair, chocolate eyes and a creamy honey and olive oil tinted skin. A dream child. Leon's dream child. A little girl that captured not only Leon's heart, but filled all his waking hours. From day one, Debbie was Daddy's girl. With Debbie in his arms, Leon developed almost overnight, into a caring, compassion, understanding, loving father. The transition was astounding. All these wonderful new traits he suddenly exhibited carried only one flaw. His target zone was only Debbie.

I became the built-in baby sitter/brother.

Believe it or not, for a while, I actually enjoyed it..

Bob & Debbie

I learned all the necessities such as diaper changing, dressing, spoon feeding and potting training. I also learned how loud a baby can cry, daytime or nighttime. I learned how to hold her until she fell asleep. Dorothy told me it was all good training for later in life when I had my own. Debbie prepared me for something else too.

She slept in my room with me. My previous lack of privacy made the transition easy. I now had even less privacy in my room which now was referred to as Debbie's room. Eventually we would need another bedroom. I knew Leon didn't plan on building another house. If I ever needed another reason to leave, I had a new one now.

Debbie was the only reason I stayed on as long as I did. She was a breath of fresh air in a home that had become contaminated with role playing. Dorothy played the obedient wife, lying whenever necessary to please Leon. Dressing to please Leon. Catering shamelessly to Leon's demands. Shamming to fit into the upper echelon of society. Playing the caring, loving mother. And me, lying to cover up the friends I associated with; lying about the girls I was dating, and of course, not divulging the extra monies I picked up, across from the high school, on noon hours shooting pool. The cigarettes I smoked, the sloe gin I drank and the clothes I hid throughout high school, though minor infractions, all fed from the same trough. Our family was a house of lies.

When Deborah Leone was adopted. She was a magnet for all their attentions. This was a blessing for me. I loved little Debbie. I enjoyed playing with her; watching her learn to crawl, then walk. I played with her outside, showing her off to my friends.

I remember gathering all the silver dollars that I had received on my birthday from my Grandma Rapsey. Hopefully eventually amassing enough to someday purchase a new first baseman's glove.

However, because it was Debbie's first celebrated birthday with us and I felt I needed to do something special,

I took my silver stash and purchased a sterling silver and gold locket for her. Had it engraved, with love, Big Brother Bob. She was truly a huggable, beautiful brown eyed doll.

Leon was totally enamored with her. As weeks grew into months she became his whole life. Eventually even Dorothy was pushed out of the picture. Leon's consuming passion for Debbie began to cause tensions between the two of them. The arguments began again. Debbie was far too young to know the ramifications of her relationship with Leon, but even outsiders had questioned his obsession with his little girl.

A neighbor who lived beside us made a questionable remark to Dorothy one day suggesting that Leon's attentions to Debbie seemed to shut out any room for her or Bobbie. Dorothy never noted as overly intuitive, became upset over the innuendo, and promptly made the mistake of relaying said comments to Leon, apparently in an accusatory tone.

His ballistic over-reaction to her comments, led me to make a quick and un-noticed retreat. I most definitely wanted to be elsewhere when all hell broke loose. Several hours later, silence greeted my return. Neither of them spoke to me or each other for what seemed like several days. To be honest? I enjoyed the quiet. The aftermath of their fights always provided me with periods of calmness that I truly relished.

Chapter Seventeen
Movin' On

Right or wrong, I'm out of here.

Most people have a plan in life. What they want to do. What they hope to achieve. Goals thoughtfully set and planned for. I guess my first goal out of high school was to gain total independence. Such a delusion. I've since learned that no one ever has total independence. Every person on this planet has a dependence on someone or something. My goal of independence was not so much a goal as it was a quest created by fear. I needed to get out from under Leon's total control. I wanted to find a life where I was treated as my friends were. They had parents they looked up to. Parents they could go to for help. It was too late for the parent thing, but I felt I was an okay person. There must be someone out there who would agree with me. Enter Bill and Edna Zuurhoud.

Room & Board $15.00 wk.

The summer of '55 opened to the confluence of many colliding factors. The least of which was Debbie. The pivotal factor being Leon's discovery of the educational barricade he encountered at the London Life Insurance Company. With only an eighth grade education, he had gone as far as he could go within the company. His decision to leave was followed by another decision, to leave Kitchener and return to his French roots. So, in spite of Dorothy's vehement protests, he sold out and prepared to move to Montreal. I decided it was time to avail myself of this opportunity. So I advised them that now being of legal age, I was opting out of the move. Surprising to me at the time, but not so, in retrospect, neither of them argued against my staying behind.

And so they left. For Montreal. I stayed in Kitchener. I had my independence.

I purchased my dream car, a 1939 Studebaker President. A beautiful wine colored four door sedan with stick shift on the floor. The only possessions I took with me were my clothes, piled on the back seat. A maneuver that I unfortunately repeated many times in my life.

A randomly selected ad for a room led me to a quiet street, miles away from the extravagant Westmount area. The wide, well used front porch seemed to invite me up the steps. Through the window I saw a matronly lady coming to answer the door. A new phase of my life was about to commence.

The Zuurhouds.

Edna Zuurhoud was a round faced, rather rotund middle-aged woman with a ready laugh and as I soon learned, a warm loving hug. Much like my Grandma Rapsey's. She was a wonderful cook and kept an immaculate home.

Big Bill, her husband was a gentle, caring man with sparkling eyes and a vociferous laugh. He spent five days a week in the factory and the rest of his life with his family. They had one son, Bill Junior. He was only four years older than I and he in many ways became my surrogate older brother. Their family relationship was what I had only been able to fantasize about. It was a real family and I became a part of it.

The Dominion Bank

Spring 1955, Toronto Dominion Bank

High Finance

The previous summer I had worked at the Dominion Bank in downtown Kitchener, so now in need of a full time job, I went back to the bank and was re-hired.

Made a world of new friends. Helen Levenduski, Clare Roth, Verne Koenig and of course Gerry Corlett the manager. But my new best friend was Eddie Roth.

Eddie was already a teller when I arrived. I was put on the cash book. A giant ledger wherein all the daily transaction were laboriously transcribed. It was either my penmanship or my skill with numbers, but I was very quickly promoted to fourth teller.

My station was next to Eddie's. Eddie was a Mennonite. What was affectionately known as the shiny bumper Mennonite. In the fifties the Mennonites were divided into three groups. The true ones lived a life of poverty driving only horse and buggy and absolutely no electricity. The next groups were the black bumpers. They had cars, but they painted the bumpers black. They also had electricity, but no phones or radios. They were moderately modern, but no glitz. Eddie was in the third group. Mennonite in religion, but decidedly modern in his acquisitions. His '49 Chevy was always washed and as shiny as it could possibly be. Latest style clothes and latest style girls. My kind of guy.

One of our jobs when we weren't tellering, was to make the trip across town to other banks, either bringing them bags of coins or picking up the same for our bank. It was usually good for a couple of hours out of the bank and a special reward after hours when we checked the trunk of Eddie's car for spilled and forgotten coins. Each trip netted us between two and seven dollars. Quite a haul for guys earning less than thirty dollars a week! Life was sweet. Made some money each week, paid my rent, and spent the rest. In my first year I had three pay raises bringing my weekly check to thirty-two, fifty. Wow! And beer was only a nickel a glass. I thought I had the world by the proverbial tail.

Chapter Eighteen
Young Love

Angela Marie Diebolt

She was 24 weeks and three days older than me. The lure of the mystery and intrigue of an older woman overpowered any limited common sense that I may have had. I was smitten. Angela Marie. The name alone suggested adoration, or at the least a genuflect. If she'd wore a flowing white robe crowned with a soft golden glow above her head, I would have probably washed her feet with my hair. Teenager in love. If the world could harness that power, mankind would never again need food, clothing or shelter. Such is the greatness of eighteen year olds in love.

Unfortunately, such power can be a negative force as well. Sometimes it just takes a while to manifest itself amidst all the blooms of love.

Leon and Dorothy had barely shed the dust of Kitchener when I immersed myself in the world of newfound freedoms. Beer drinking, smoking, shooting pool, staying out until the early morning hours. Heading to Niagara or Buffalo for wild unfettered parties. The single life was all I'd hoped it would be and more!

The Kitchener pub scene provided all the female company I could need or want. Sometimes, perhaps just a tad too much. But the occasional hangover was usually assuaged by the memories of what or who caused it. Each day brought new opportunities and new adventures. But sadly, like day old beer and stale cigarettes the thrill started to wane. Even at eighteen I could see the writing on the wall. I'd heard enough stories about how Ralph ended up. I had seen first hand the lifestyle/relationship of Jim and Gwen. I wasn't exactly clear on what I was looking for, but I knew my current path would not lead me there. Dating Angela brought about serious change in my life.

Emil & Rose Diebolt

Her mother Rose and father Emil welcomed me in their home. I had dated Angie in high school, so most of the family already knew me. They reminded me of "June bug's" family. They didn't preach and they didn't condemn. I joined them for meals and eventually joined in, on occasion for their evening prayers. They were big on prayers.

Emil's brother was a priest, Rose's sister was a nun and Angie's older sister was a high school principal in St John's Catholic School. I never did grasp the concept of repeating the same prayer words over and over again. Like the big guy won't answer till you've inundated him with several hundred hail Marys. Come on folks, these carved in stone prayer rules are brought to you by the same guys who said if you eat meat on Friday, you're going to hell, then after they received too much flack from the real people, they relented and said it was now okay, because we've created a new rule. These sentiments, I managed to keep to myself while in their house. When in Rome, etc etc.

I think the most prominent feature; about the Diebolt clan was that they were a family. They had family values. Christmas, birthdays, anniversaries, all were celebrated by all the family.

As Angela's boyfriend, I was invited to all the parties. I developed a taste for pig tails, home made sausage, neck bones soup, blood sausage, and sauerkraut. I never did take to Emil's Limburger cheese though. But I thoroughly relished the idea of being part of their family. I found acceptance. Perhaps not actual blessings, but at least acceptance. More than I'd ever experienced at home. Acceptance is superior to endurance.

Chapter Nineteen
The Studebaker

June 6th. 1956

Though Emil and Rose treated me very well, they were never enamored with the idea of having me for a son-in-law. Who could blame them? Nineteen-year-old boy, thinking he's a man, working in a bank for $32.50 a week and paying fifteen of that for room and board. And a 1938 Studebaker that was on its last legs.

The Studebaker in its demise actually was the catalyst that pushed me into making the biggest decision of my life.

My car was truly a workhorse. The engine was a straight eight. The car was four thousand pounds of armor gage steel. Mileage was unimportant as gas was cheap. But oil became more and more important to me with each passing mile. The old Studebaker would use three quarts of oil every fifteen miles. Great clouds of blue smoke billowed out behind me as I ferried this monster across town.

Angela was quite embarrassed to be seen in it. But given the alternative, two or three bus transfers, she would ride with her head down, hoping no one would recognize her. A rather futile effort since we left a smoke trail visible for three miles.

After a date one night, on the way home, the transmission made a loud clang and we slowly drifted to a stop. I ascertained that we had lost third gear. But I discovered that I could still use second. So I managed to carry her home in grand style, at twenty-five miles an hour.

The next day, I lost second gear too. I was due at Angela's for supper, so with fingers crossed I left Zuurhouds and headed across town in my only gear, first. I almost made it too. Then first gear died, five blocks from her house. In desperation I tried reverse. It still worked! Five blocks in reverse for almost a half an hour. Angie's brother and father were outside laughing when I backed up in front of their house.

I called a junk man who paid me twenty-five dollars for it and towed it away. I used the money for a down payment on an engagement ring.

Popcorn Engagement

A few days later in a movie theater in downtown Kitchener, in the dark I slipped the engagement ring into Angela's popcorn. We thus became engaged and she commenced perusing the calendar. June 6th 1956, was the chosen date. Wow! Less than six weeks away.

Emil booked the reception hall and arranged the beer and wine. Rose arranged the church and the dinner. Angie started choosing bridesmaids and gowns. My job? Well, I started thinking, and sweating. Perhaps this was one of those decisions made in haste and repented in leisure. Prudence was still an option. Prudence? I thought that was a girl's name. And so Angela and I charged forward into the fields of marital bliss. Both of us nurturing unspoken doubts.

Chapter Twenty
Time to draw back and re-think

There are two major decisions in a young man's life which when made without aforethought or available experience will profoundly affect his life from that decision forward. The first is not getting married. The second is getting married.

My knee jerk reaction to the date of June 6th being a real date for my real wedding instigated some long serious conversations between Angela and me. Pros and cons were discussed and weighed as they should have been done before the announcement. Turns out we both were laboring under heavy misgivings. The end result was that we decided to delay setting a wedding date till sometime in the future.

The Diebolts, in spite of all the time and money spent in preparation, were surprisingly cordial about the cancellations they now faced. Perhaps the spark of maturity shown by the canceling made up for lack of common sense and maturity shown in the first decision.

I needed to make some plans for some tomorrows and all the ones to follow. My only skills were in marketing. Actually I wasn't even skilled in marketing; I was just a teen-age salesman.

After the demise of my Studebaker, I desperately needed transportation. My work history wasn't long enough to qualify for a car loan. To my rescue came Reuben, Angie's older brother. Reuben loaned me six hundred dollars to buy a car. I had a golden opportunity to buy a car at under market value.

The Meteor

It was a 1953 metallic green Meteor. It was in perfect shape except for one minor problem. It was owned by a man who had only one leg. The left one. He operated the gas with a lever on the steering column. And he braked with his left foot. The brake petal shaft had been bent across to where the clutch normally would have been. Thereby necessitating using my right foot for the gas and my left one for the brake. Hence the lower than market price. Shouldn't be a problem. I used my left foot for the brake lots of times.

And so I bought it.

I had owned this beautiful car for about two weeks when I was heading downtown for an appointment. I pulled across traffic and over to the far inside lane. As I crept along the curb lane watching the red light ahead of me, I was poised to slam the accelerator to the floor at just the right moment and surge ahead of all those in the other lane, thereby putting me at the front of the traffic. Unfortunately, the lead car in the center lane signaled a semi in the opposing lane to go ahead and make his left turn. Wouldn't have been a problem if there had been a brake petal where I repeated slammed my foot to the floorboards. Instead, I T-boned the semi directly into his saddle tanks. I survived better than the car. I had cuts on my forehead and nose and bleeding shin and knee. The car had to be towed to a garage. Ontario immediately cancelled my insurance necessitating the removal of my license plate, pending proof of liability insurance. A chore made decidedly more difficult by my lack of transportation.

All of which helped propel me into another rash decision.

I called Montreal.

Chapter Twenty-One
Montreal

Back into fray the fool rode

To say Leon and Dorothy were not pleased to hear my voice from that payphone would be a gross understatement. I humbly told them of the cancelled engagement, the car accident and my severe lack of financial wherewithal. I submissively requested a place to stay while I located employment in Montreal. I conceded to his every condition. I suspected this might turn out to be my most colossal mistake yet.

The next day, I sold the car to the garage where it was stored. Paid off Reuben and asked a good friend Laverne Sherk to drive and me to Toronto where I boarded a train for Point Claire. Six hours later I walked into the Perras house in Beaconsfield, Quebec.

Dorothy's cool greeting did nothing to allay the misgivings I had about my latest decision. She walked me up a narrow flight of stairs to the attic. At the top she pointed to a small room and reminded me that they had not planned on any company so this would have to do. The small window, bare floors, single bed and chest of drawers contrasted tremendously with the extravagant furnishings in the main house.

But, I thought, beggars can't be choosy.

The house was a frame two story, second floor as yet unfinished, on a large lot in a private gated community. Across from the front door were a large tennis court and a grassy park area ending at the shore of the St Lawrence River. Moored at the docks were half a dozen boats of varying sizes. The neighbors were all high level executives. Presidents, owners and high rollers. Leon had at last achieved his dream. Living high in the thin air. Except that when he arrived here, he was basically unemployed. Not poor, just no visible occupation. Retired insurance executive seemed to fit.

His first venture out of the industry he had been employed in for twenty years was his fifty thousand dollar investment into a Travel Agency. He discovered all too quickly why the previous owners were so anxious to sell. This foray into owning his own business was a financial disaster. He probably enjoyed the perks more than the business. Availing himself of the free flights on the commercial airlines certainly made an interesting talking point at the proverbial cocktail parties. But alas, the life of booking other people's vacation trips didn't fit in with his idea of a semi retired executive.

Incidentally several years later I financed, contracted and built a half million dollar club in Tallahassee using what the vernacular of the day called O.P.M. Meaning "other people's money". Fortunately the club made money, but if it had not and had it gone south, I would not have had to bear the entire financial loss myself. Ergo, the preservation of one's assets through the assiduous use of O.P.M. (other people's money). I mention this, because in a conversation some years later, he severely chastised and berated me for utilizing the O.P.M. financing methods, presenting his example of his losing fifty thousand dollars of his own money as a more ethical way of doing business. I've never understood his obscure rational.

His next venture utilized his talent with words and figures. He entered the world of industrial real estate development. He had found his niche in his world. He was sixty years old. He excelled at it and very soon he actually fit quite well in the financial community to which he had so long aspired. Six decades after leaving Ottawa, he had proven that he had what it took, to finally realize his dream. He was a financially successful real estate developer.

T. Eaton Company

After humbly explaining my series of misadventures that ended with my landing on their doorstep, I commenced my search for suitable employment.

Jobs were plentiful. Transportation was not. Rather than be faced with an unemployed son lounging around the house, Leon talked to his next-door neighbor, who just happened to be the President of the T. Eaton Company, Montreal.

They apparently had a manager's training program in which I could participate. It was an interesting concept. The new employee would work for one week in each and every department in the store. From women's garments to hardware. I actually enjoyed it. A new department every week left very little time to get bored. And the Montreal women dressed with a touch of class I'd never seen in Kitchener!

But the commute was a killer. Not too bad during the summer, but the sub zero Montreal winters was a deal breaker.

Beaconsfield was, by train, forty-five minutes from downtown Montreal. It meant leaving the house at six, walk to the entrance of Gables Court, the grandiose name for the enclosure in which the Perras's lived, wait by the side of the highway for a bus to ride to Point Claire and then ride the train to the Montreal station. Walk the remaining eight blocks to the T. Eaton Company. Then reverse the procedure and arrive home at seven o'clock in the evening.

My home life was basically mundane. Leon still had his red leather throne, only now recovered in brown leather. Subtler but still his command center. Most of the few conversations we had usually took place in front of his chair. Except for one especially interesting one.

The final conversation

Every morning Leon would get up about five-thirty and do some form of mild exercise in the living room. For company more than camaraderie he invited me to join him. After fifteen minutes we would move to the kitchen table and drink our coffee and smoke a cigarette. Yes, by now they had accepted that I smoked. I remember well, Dorothy's snide remark when I first pulled one out shortly after arriving. "Oh so we're smoking now are we"? Struck me as a stupid thing to say, as I blew a stream of smoke across the room.

As we drank our coffee, Leon looked at me for a long time, finally setting his cup down and leaned forward as if to tell me a secret. "You and Angela seem to be sharing a lot of correspondence lately. Are you considering re-activating that relationship"? It took me by surprise and I stammered that I date all kinds of girls around here, and why would I do that? He reiterated, "That's what I'm asking you. It seems to me that you have a lot of girlfriends, a good job and a fair amount of money. Why would you even be corresponding with her"? I felt anger welling inside me, reminiscent of the Kitchener days when he ran every detail of my life. I held my tongue in check till his next remark. "I want all ties to her broken off. You may continue to live under my roof, but she will not be a part of your life".

Wham, there it was again. His way, his rules, his decisions, his controls. I saw only the negative. I couldn't see the positive aspects. Living in a beautiful home, working in a privileged position, meeting and dating exciting women, taking in the latest club acts in downtown Montreal. None of this registered. My argumentative response was to advise him that it was my life and I'll date or correspond with whomever I want. His reply spurred me on to make the second most crucial mistake of my first twenty years. Fine I said, then I'll move out. "When", he asked? In a couple of weeks I said. "No" he replied, anger welling up inside him. "You're out tonight"!

I came home that evening to find Leon standing just inside the back door. Beside him, a brown paper shopping bag, a small suitcase and my guitar were stacked by the door. "There's a bus to Montreal in forty minutes, he said. Be on it". I reminded him that it was fifteen below zero and snowing. He reminded me of our original telephone conversation. It was his way or the highway. My choice.

Outside the Gables Court stone wall, at the side of the road, I sat upon the suitcase and watched the snow pile up on my guitar. The next bus wasn't due for thirty-five minutes. In my pocket I recounted my cash. Forty-three dollars! Then I fingered the last letter Angela sent me in which she pleaded with me to come back home to her. She was about to get her wish. I spent the night in Montreal at the YMCA. I telephoned Angela. I don't know if I slept at all that night, but I do remember that I was an hour early for the train to Toronto. I remember thinking, am I nuts? Perhaps Leon's actions weren't just his reaction to my obstinacy. Maybe I should re-think this decision.

Nope. Too late. Can't back down.

Bad decision!!

Chapter Twenty-Two
Kitchener

The Entire Diebolt Clan & One Perras

Memories fifty years old are at best, hazy. I remember that Angela wore white. I wore a blue blazer and gray slacks. The church was divided by "his" side and "her" side. Her side was at capacity, about 90 relatives and girl friends. My side looked like someone had hung a wet paint sign on it. Was this unbalance a portent of things to come? Was Angela going through the metamorphous to become a Perras or was I being mutated into a Diebolt? At that time, who thought of such things? I simply thought that I finally had a family. Different names, different religions, and different values, but none the less, a family, who I assumed, if only because I married the baby of the family, cared about me. And for a while, they did.

As a young man of twenty, it was amazing how little I understood about responsibilities. Coming from a decade of tutelage under the "Leon Perras Rules Committee", one would think I would have developed into the epitome of mature responsibility. Maybe I resented Leon's yoke of responsibilities placed around my neck and simply couldn't wait to toss it away. In any case I did not carry the mantle of marriage and or responsibilities very well.

Sides were drawn very early in our marriage. Angela wanted her own house, garden and children. She wanted quiet times with her friends. She continued to be the baby of the Diebolt clan, thriving on the unending caring and attentions. She asked very little of life to be happy. All of her brothers and sisters, aunts and uncles, first and second cousins, all resided in and around Kitchener-Waterloo. Half her family worked at a local plant and most would eventually retire from that same company. This was her plan for us.

This was not my plan for us!

For almost a year I had worked in downtown Montreal, commerce and economic center for Canada. Thirty storied skyscrapers looming over a downtown filled with swarming, hustling throngs, all making their way in the exciting world that I had only dreamed of back in Kitchener.

Evenings in clubs with Marty Robbins singing a White Sport Coat and Chubby Checkers doing his Twist.

Week-ends horseback riding in the Laurention Mountain foothills. The Chateau Champlain Hotel, Dorval Airport, and the mighty St Lawrence River, all beckoned me to partake of their wonders.

This is what I spoke of to Angela when we talked of our future. This is what I felt the future held for me. She didn't agree. She wanted less. I wanted more. Neither of us right. Neither of us wrong. The only error was made when we didn't discuss it at greater length before we entered the church.

Paths Divided

Within months our paths had already branched and the etching of the stone begun. It was obvious that the course would not be altered. I never knew just how much my future had been preordained.

From the top: Bonny, Shelly, Cindy & Terry

Angela and I decided that it would be in the best interest for all if we parted amicably.

There have been reams and reams written on the subject of divorce and its effect on the participants. More importantly how it affects each life. My children had their lives torn apart by my leaving. Our family ceased to exist.

The children blamed themselves. Angela and I blamed each other. There are not words to describe the pain the children endured with the departure of their father. They knew little of the fears faced by Angela who for twelve years had a spouse to share personal and financial challenges. No one will ever know the pain I felt each morning when I went to work at construction sites in Florida, and saw the faces of my four daughters before me. Life is full of choices. Angela and I thought we made the correct choice. That choice has been questioned many times by many people.

For the next three decades I entered into and exited from uncounted and barely remembered relationships. I criss-crossed the entire U.S.A. racking up thousands of miles selling franchises for ARCO's photo voltaic division. I sold products door to door and business to business. I designed and built a private social club in Tallahassee. I owned advertising agencies and television production companies in Denver. In Clearwater I owned and retired from The Perras Publishing Group. I grasped every opportunity that presented itself. Always with the optimism that this one will be even better than the last. Some were, some weren't. I capitalized on so many opportunities, but I never really enjoyed the successes because of my obsession with seeking Leon's approval. Approval that would never come.

At twenty-eight thousand square feet, a half million dollar club that I designed built and managed elicited a curt, "not very big is it"?

Steve Allen & Bob Perras

My Denver television production company that produced half hour industrials for major corporations as well as a television episode of Meeting of the Minds with Steve Allen, was summed up by Leon with "you have no background in the business, do something you have experience in". Radio stations and newspapers in Denver ran ads created by my agencies. My publishing company in Clearwater published directories for contractors and builders throughout the state of Florida. The latest endeavors were all met with stony silence. Probably because at the time he was in his eighties and really didn't care.

But I did. All I ever wanted, was just once to hear a note of proud; a smile for my achievements. A vocal well done son. Leon died without ever acquiescing.

I was always searching. Every time I thought I'd struck the mother lode, it turned out to be pyrite. Fog and mirrors. The money wasn't enough. The relationships never lasted. Nothing was truly fulfilling. But I never stopped forging ahead. I knew that somewhere another shiny penny would pop up giving me one more opportunity.

Eventually after a half century of pursuit, I finally realized that all my efforts for success were really driven by the need for Leon Perras's approval. I finally gave up chasing that impossible dream and accepted that Leon would never openly show approval.

But by now too many opportunities for personal happiness had been cast aside in my relentless pursuit. People who cared for me, tired and left. Friends cautioned me that business makes for poor bedmates. Relatives long since estranged gave up inviting me to share in their lives. I became a self created pariah.

Four decades later, I was in a restaurant, in Clearwater Florida, sipping coffee and lining up pennies on the table. Which one represents my next adventure? Bad choices had left my life in shambles. Once again I would have to re-build everything in my life. All that I had achieved in the last two decades evaporated. Because of one bad choice! Did fate have one more penny of opportunity for me?

I was in a somber mood, vacillating between self pity and well -- more self pity, when a ray of sunshine caressed this vision walking towards me. It reflected from the silver in her hair and actually lit up my pennies.

She sat down and said, "Hi my name is Olivia". Everything in my life just changed.

Pennies for You

While it may be presumptuous to figuratively draw a line and state that this is a fair and complete representation of my first twenty years, it's no less a waste of paper and ink to draw upon any additional episodes from the past, solely for the purpose of expatiating the story.

I believe this book thus far is a fair encapsulation of the events and people, who were in part and in varied capacities, pivotal in the shaping of who I am today. I believe everyone's personalities; traits, drives and ambitions are created and nurtured during these fertile years. The path chosen in one's life is basically traceable to physical, moral and intellectual experiences. Yet it is not necessary to embrace the negatives in life. One must transcend the bumps and curves in the road of life.

Pennies are not merely the coin of the realm. They're symbols. The penny is ubiquitous. It's saved in the poorest pocket and ignored in the richest purse. They're hoarded in jars and ignored on the pavements. They're everywhere. Just take time to look. Find them, and use them to represent the myriad positive opportunities presented to you every day. Bobbie's pennies became a bright spot in my life.

One small moment in time, which I remember and draw upon as my credo, to bridge life's roadblocks, in my never ending pursuit of new opportunities.

Epilogue

This book was written in part, to satisfy an unfulfilled ambition of mine, and in part, as a thinly disguised ego trip.

After a long, (far longer than anticipated) and frequently blessed (perhaps lucky) lifetime, I feel I have failed to leave any kind of indelible mark behind. Not meaning statues or monuments or any other self gratifying epitaph, but rather, something that says, "this was Bob Perras; it's who he was and what he did with his life". It does not attempt to answer nor even to ask the question, "was it all worthwhile?". It does not seek praise nor offer apologies. It is simply, my story.

It is my sincerest hope that someday in the future, one or more of my four daughters, might have sufficient curiosity to sit down and read about who and what their father was, and what he did with his life. Perhaps, many years further on, one or more of my many grandchildren and great grandchildren may also be rather curious about their heritage.

This effort represents seven decades in the making and several years in the writing. None of which would have happened were it not for my wonderful wife, who inspired me and kept prodding me with unending patience and encouragement whenever I faltered.

On behalf of whoever reads this and hopefully enjoys it, I gratefully extend my thanks, to you, Liv for its creation.